From Humble Beginnings

Best wishes to
Anne Veevers!

Enjoy.

From Humble Beginnings: Songs of a Native Son

William Franklin Andrews

Foreword by Mary Trim Anderson

Arranged and edited by Thomas Brent Andrews

Published by Chronic 𝄞 Discontent Books
Franklin, Tennessee

FROM HUMBLE BEGINNINGS

This is a work of non-fiction poems and stories. The people and places in this book actually exist, and the author expresses his sincere thanks to those friends mentioned here for being the kind of people one would want to write poems about, and remember. He also wishes to thank his wife Carolyn and friend Glenna Jacobs for reading and commenting on the manuscript, Mary Trim Anderson for writing the foreword, and the sponsors who helped make this book possible.

© 2005 William Frank Andrews and Chronic Discontent Books

Published 2005 by Chronic Discontent Books
Thomas Brent Andrews, Publisher
P.O. Box 1514
Franklin, Tennessee 37065

All rights reserved. No part of this book may be used or reproduced in any manner whatsoever without written permission, except in the case of brief quotations embodied in critical articles or reviews.

Printed 2005 by CafePress.com in the United States of America

ISBN 0-9767056-1-3

Cover designed by Jeff Hottle

Contents designed by Ginny Andrews

The cover photo shows the author at about 13 years old, riding "Molly" on a Williamson County farm where he lived with his grandfather, a tenant farmer or "sharecropper" named Norman Sullivan who could drive mules and turn a phrase with the best of them; his grandmother Mona Sullivan; his many aunts and uncles; his sister Jean; and domestic animals of all descriptions. The short stories "The Night the House Almost Burned Down," "A Shirt Named Eugene," and "Snowball the Orphan Lamb" were gathered on this fertile Tennessee farm. The poem "Death of a Great House" documents its sad fate.

The Chronic Discontent Books logo is borrowed from *Ancient Sichuan and the Unification of China*, by Steven F. Sage, State University of New York Press, 1992. The bone inscription is believed to be approximately 3,200 years old. Writes Sage: "Conjecture relates this eye to a legendary version of Shu origins mentioning a 'vertical-eyed man' (*zong mu zhi ren*), figuratively perhaps meaning a 'man of vision.'"

This book is dedicated to my loving and always faithful wife Carolyn Smithson Andrews, who for poetic reasons is affectionately known as "Martha."

Table of Contents

Foreword .... *xi*

Prologue: Mule Barn Blues *1*

Part 1: Light *3*

    STEPPING STONES 5

    SEEDS 6

    FLOWERS 7

    THE LOVE NEST 8

    THE ONE-LEGGED DUCK 10

    THE BELLS 11

    NATURE 12

    THE SWITCH 13

    THE TRIAL 14

    SNOW 16

    LIFE 17

    THE SUN 18

    THE RENDEZVOUS 19

    LIFE'S POKER GAME 20

    SAND CASTLES 22

    UNTITLED 23

    LITTLE BOY OF COMITAN 24

    POLITIKIN' 25

Part 2: Franklin *27*

    MY HOME TOWN 29

    DOWNTOWN FRANKLIN 30

MEETING OF THE WATERS.................................31

HOMES OF THE MASTER 33

OUR MONUMENT..34

MY HOMETOWN BANK.................................35

FASHION CLEANERS 37

LORI'S BOOK STORE 39

LAZY SUMMER...40

JUST LIKE YESTERDAY 42

THE PEPPER PATCH 44

DEATH OF A GREAT HOUSE 45

Part 3: Hometown People.............................. *47*

FOR 'PEK' GUNN AT EIGHTY........................49

FRANK LYNCH – MY HERO 50

MY TRIBUTE TO MISS EULALIE JEFFERSON.........51

TO AMY AND DAVID 53

RCT. SCOTT A BURCHYETT – SOON TO BE A U.S. MARINE...54

ANNA CLAIRE SMITHSON.............................55

SISTER JEAN...56

TO MARY ANN AT FORTY 57

MY SISTER'S HOUSE.....................................58

MY TRIBUTE TO DANNY DUKE 59

A TRIBUTE TO HAYWOOD COLE 60

TO DONALD PIERCE AT FIFTY......................62

TO DONALD H. PIERCE DEPARTED LOVED ONE ..63

FOR MOM – MY SPECIAL MOTHER-IN-LAW 65

TO JIMMY SMITHSON AT FORTY - 1988 67

BRIAN 68

STEPHANIE 69

PUSHER TRAINS (COWAN, TENNESSEE) 70

THE SHRINER...72

CLARENCE JOHNSON 73

NOBLE CARSON, 1905 - 1990 74

SUMMER 76

Part 4: Trades..*77*

THE PLUMBER..79

THE VEGETABLE MAN 80

PAINTERS 81

THE SECRETARY 82

THE FARMER'S PLIGHT 83

THE LEADER 84

THE REALTOR 86

ALL AS ONE 88

THE CARPENTER 89

Part 5: "My wife, my children, my world.".....................*95*

CAROLYN (1956) 97

TWEEDLE-DEE-DEE 98

LOVERS...99

TO A FARAWAY LOVE 100

KING FOR A DAY...101

TWENTY-ONE YEARS..102

TWENTY-FIVE YEARS 103

'MARTHA' 105

LOVE SONG TO MARTHA...............................106

HOMES OF MY HEART 107

MY SHIP 108

MY CHILDREN 109

TO VICTOR ON YOUR LEAVING FOR COLLEGE (AUG. 19, 1981)..110

TO VICTOR AND SUZANNE ON YOUR WEDDING (JUNE 23, 1990) 111

A FARM AT THE END OF THE ROAD 113

WILLIAM PATRICK ANDREWS (DEDICATION SUNDAY, JAN. 5, 1992)..114

HANNAH MURIEL ANDREWS (DEDICATION SUNDAY, DEC. 4, 1994)..115

WELCOME CLAIRE SUSANNAH ANDREWS (BORN MAY 31, 1997) 116

CAMPBELL JAMES ANDREWS (DEDICATION FEB. 24, 2002)..117

BETH AT TWENTY MONTHS 118

BETH 119

BECKY 120

TO BECKY AFTER SYMPHONY CONCERT.............121

TO BECKY ON YOUR LEAVING FOR COLLEGE (SEPTEMBER 1985)..122

FOR CHRISTOPHER AND BECKY STEERE (ON THEIR WEDDING DAY JAN. 26, 1991)........................124

JESSE'S SHOES..126

JESSE'S MEADOW..127

CHARLES FRANKLIN STEERE 128

BRENT (FOURTH BIRTHDAY) 129

BRENT (THIRD GRADE) 130

TO BRENT AT 15 (ALMOST 15) 131

FOR BRENT AND GINNY 132

PRICE STALLARD 134

WELCOME VIOLET 135

MY CHILDREN ARE MY GIFT TO GOD 136

GOING HOME 138

THORNHILL (1983) 139

TOMORROW I'll BRING FLOWERS...........................140

Part 6: War...................................... *141*

A CRY FOR PEACE...................................143

LETTER FROM A SOLDIER 145

WELCOME HOME – THE PROUD AND THE BRAVE
...................................147

OUR FAMILY (JULY 28, 1996) 149

Part 7: Three Stories...................................... *151*

A SHIRT NAMED EUGENE 153

SNOWBALL THE ORPHAN LAMB 156

THE NIGHT THE HOUSE ALMOST BURNED DOWN
...................................159

Part 8: Broke...................................... *161*

MY TREASURE SHIP 163

CHRISTMAS 164

ODE TO A SON OF A B----! 166

FRANK 167

DARK TIDES 168

TAKING IT EASY 169

BUSTED 170

MY PRAYER 171

Part 9: Writing the Sounds of Night *173*

THE BOTTOM 175

HELL 176

THOUGHTS FROM A SMALL COUNTRY GRAVEYARD 177

GENTLE WINDS 178

A PATCH OF EARTH 179

I KNOW A PLACE 180

EIGHTY-SIX CROSSES 181

MEDITATIONS 183

DON'T GET HOOKED ON DRUGS 184

THE HUNTER 185

THE VOICE OF THE UNBORN 186

A CHOICE OF LIFE 187

THE MASTER'S FEET 188

THE FARMER'S HOME 189

SPECULATIONS 190

Part 10: Reminiscing *191*

REMINISCING 193

BAREFOOT BOY 194

GRANDPA 195

GRANDMOTHER 197

MOTHER 198

CHILDHOOD MEMORIES 199

A CHILD FOR A DAY 201

Epilogue: Lines from God *203*

About the Author *205*

Sponsors *207*

Foreword

In all my years of teaching and throughout the years of my retirement, my life has been blessed with the continued friendships with former students and by their kind remarks that I had a positive influence in their lives. It has always been a special pleasure for me to see the written work of one of these past students in print, whether it be verse, fiction or reflection of days gone by.

Such is the case with Frank Andrews.

One can see at a glance the maturing of boy to man. One reads of life experiences – his, or others' – issues of morality, sage advice, and especially of his observation of and appreciation for the beauty of the world around us.

Frank has succeeded in a number of life's roles – son, husband, father, businessman. Yet, his poetic nature always seemed to find expression. His request that I write the foreword for this publication I deem a compliment; it is my pleasure to have a small part in his latest achievement. To quote the author,

> *"Using all the cards you're given*
> *Is how success in life is made."*

Mary Trim Anderson
Franklin, Tennessee
June 2005

William Frank Andrews

Prologue: Mule Barn Blues

Out in the country just ten miles from town;
A part of Ft. Carson is tumbling down.
Built back in 'forty for mules not for men;
The 'RED DEVILS' moved out and the Medics moved in.
Someone please thank those wonderful souls
For being so generous to give us this HOLE.
For so many things they left without charge
The mud in the barracks; the sludge in the yard,
The rocks in the path, the crud in the street,
KP with 'ole Barta just three times a week.
Now I'm not complaining so don't take me wrong
I've got <u>CHANCE</u> and not <u>CHOICE</u> so no matter how long:
If these MULE BARNS need cleaning I'll stick to my song;
What's this stuff I'm sweeping; is it ding, dung or dong?
The duty's not bad if you like to cut weeds,
Sweep out the barns or be OJT'ed.
It's just three miles from the main PX.
But they bought me some shoes "So well what the heck."
I just can't get over those infantry boys,
Moving and leaving these wonderful joys.
Perhaps it will all come clear someday –
In the meantime I'll just forget I'm RA.
These MULE BARN BLUES have gotten me down,
Only ten miles from the nearest town;
Cracks in the windows; bugs in the walls
I can't figure why I ENLISTED at ALL.
Just nine hundred days and it'll all be over
I'll be a wreck, a BUM, and a ROVER;

From Humble Beginnings

I'm sure it's quite obvious; I think you can see –
These MULE BARN BLUES are killing me.

Signed "THE PHANTOM," 1962, Ft. Carson, CO

Part 1: Light

William Frank Andrews

STEPPING STONES

Stepping stones in waters blue;
Let me cross o'er to places new.
As I pass o'er I will find time
To let your waters clear my mind.

How you were placed I do not know,
By tides you were tossed to and fro.
Then side-by-side you chanced to land
As if you were placed there by man.

Don't trick me as so oft' before
And roll as I start to cross o'er.
Hold tight like leeches to the sand
Until my feet are on dry land.

So long you have been pushed around,
And soon you will be washed on down
By tides that move on to the sea;
That's why these words I speak to thee.

This is the first poem that I ever remember writing and keeping. I was about nine years old.

From Humble Beginnings

SEEDS

Gently,
In slumber
Lie seeds of Harvest,
Destined
To burst
And bring forth life.

E're warm comes
To earth again.

William Frank Andrews

FLOWERS

Oh! Flowers of green valleys
Where lieth your unseen strength?
You who waltz for hours
Breathlessly!

Joyfully
You bask in summer's gaiety,
Never crying for tomorrow
When winter's sting will kill you
Mercilessly!

From Humble Beginnings

THE LOVE NEST

He could not find the zipper on
His pants that fateful night;
Her husband standing with a gun –
His face just froze in fright.

This lady had enticed him so
With words of wit and charm.
"My husband's out of town tonight
And it will do no harm.

"You'll only stay a little while,
And leave before it's late."
But in his mind he knew so well
That he was tempting fate.

As best he could he dressed himself.
His life passed in review;
And all good deeds that he had done
He realized were few.

What seemed so good a while ago
Disaster now doth seem;
This lady who had charmed him so
Now was an empty dream.

The hammer on the gun did click

William Frank Andrews

Explosion ripped the air –
And all of hell had broken loose
Within the love nest fair.

And now beneath a tombstone lies
Two lovers 'neath the sod.
A jealous husband sent them home
One night to meet their God.

The moral to this story is
"Don't choose to mess around."
But if you do just make dang sure
The husband's out of town.

January 23, 1995

From Humble Beginnings

THE ONE-LEGGED DUCK

Did you ever see a one-legged duck
On a pond where turtles had been?
Splashing and sunning his troubles away
As if he had two legs again?

Well a one-legged duck is friendly because
He tries but can't run away.
He limps along and swims half as fast
As his two-legged friend by-the-way.

If you ever see a one-legged duck,
On a pond just flailing away;
Remember you are his two-legged friend
Without any troubles today.

For if you could be a duck for a day
With only one leg for a while;
You never would frown ever again
Your face would break out in a smile.

For Brent, March 16, 1984

William Frank Andrews

THE BELLS

'Twas Christmas morn, the bells did ring,
Across the silent way,
A call to every girl and boy
That this is Christmas day!

All through the day, from birth of dawn
Came softly to my ear;
The mellow note of Christmas song
To bring me Christmas cheer.

So merry Christmas each of you
I trust and have no fear;
That you will have through Christ the King,
A glorious New Year.

From Humble Beginnings

NATURE

When dewdrops kiss a rose in spring,
And trickle down the vine;
When we've felt winter's last dread sting
Then we drink nature's wine.

When up a mountain bold we've hiked
And touched a fragrant cloud –
Then we've seen nature and we like
To sing our praises loud.

Nature's free so hold it long,
There's still enough for me.
I can't conceive nature's song.
It charms me constantly.

Wake up early see the dawn!
Watch the flowers grow!
Watch the mother deer and fawn,
Graze in the meadow low.

Pick all the flowers in the woods
The lilies in the dale.
But don't take me from nature's goods
'Twould cause my heart to fail.

William Frank Andrews

THE SWITCH

The warden called me up today,
Said, "Wonder could you serve?
I sure do have a job for you,
That takes a lot of nerve."

I asked him what this job could pay.
I was so down on luck.
I never asked the nature of
This way to make a buck.

He said, "It pays a little bit,
I know you won't get rich;
But you'll have lots of fun my boy –
You get to pull the switch!"

I said, "I'd like to have that job,
I'll try to do it well.
I've always had a craving, sir,
To send a crook to Hell."

August 26, 1996

From Humble Beginnings

THE TRIAL

He came to court so cleanly shaven.
His clothes looked oh-so-neat.
He walked in handcuffs past the bar,
And there he took his seat.

"The charge is murder," says the judge,
"Now tell me how you plea."
"Not guilty," says the handcuffed man,
"And this kind sir you'll see."

The prosecutor tells the story –
Exactly how the victim died.
"The people beg for justice, sir!"
Unto the court he cried.

Defense attorney wisely pleads
The jury listens, too.
"I want to prove this man's a lamb,
No murder he could do.

"In all his years no single mark
Now stands against his name,
And in our town he's known by all,
And he treats them all the same.

William Frank Andrews

"The crime this man could not commit;
I'll prove he wasn't there.
And gentlemen of the jury,
I know you'll treat him fair."

Through all the day the trial did rage.
The jury listened well;
And when the day at last was done
"Not guilty," they did tell.

And so somewhere out there tonight
Someone is running free.
It seems defense has won the case
Against the prosecutor's plea.

And justice once again is served
By twelve men standing tall.
Don't shirk your jury duty when
By chance you get the call.

January 7, 1985

From Humble Beginnings

SNOW

Today the snow came;
Gently it sifted from leaden skies
Chilling both man and summer's tree –

Those shiftless feebles who chanced to leave
       Their winter frock at home!

I cannot carry a bundle of clothes
To chance being warm e're it snows.

For who can tell when summer's mountain will suddenly
       Yield its first fall of snow!

William Frank Andrews

LIFE

Moving slowly
In a warm nest of love
Life begins.
Count the heartbeat.
Feel the stir of life
In the Mother's womb.

Years later
In a world that's cold
Life ends.
Read the record.
Count the blessings
Of life.

From Humble Beginnings

THE SUN

I wonder where the sun comes from,
Or where it goes at night.
I'd like to follow it around
And see the pretty sights.

I'd stay awake my whole life thru
And never go to sleep.
'Cause now it seems my life is spent
Always counting sheep.

William Frank Andrews

THE RENDEZVOUS

It started out so innocently;
He never really loved her at all.
She just needed a shoulder;
And he was just waiting to fall.

The rendezvous came out so easily;
Not planned; it just happened that way.
He was alone in the city;
And she was just looking to play.

The night was made for the moment;
With millions of stars up above;
Two people in reckless abandon;
No shame and no semblance of love.

But now comes the time of accounting;
Too bad that they had to get laid;
She now has a brand new baby;
And he has a bad case of AIDS.

From Humble Beginnings

LIFE'S POKER GAME

Five young men were playing poker;
Five-card stud the standard flair;
Nothing wild – just plain-gut poker;
Nickels, dimes to clear the air.

Names somehow seem unimportant
Just the kind you've seen before.
Ace high card won't win much money;
Trips to win could make it more.

Deuces cheap are on the table;
Need an ace to make a straight;
Comes a jack to put you out;
Winning now will have to wait.

All of life you're playing poker.
Aces won't come every time.
Play it cool with what is dealt you
Then you'll always do just fine.

If you feel you're dealt a loser,
For a shuffle you may call.
For each card you pay a nickel;
And that's not too much at all.

William Frank Andrews

Remember winning combinations
Sometimes dealt and never played;
Using all the cards you're given
Is how success in life is made.

From Humble Beginnings

SAND CASTLES

Build a sand castle.
Carefully mold the sand
To make it look for-real.
Watch the waves
Roll higher
To kill the fairest dream
Of a sand-builder.

Walk slowly beside the sea.
Feel the ooze of sand
Between small toes.
Watch the breakers roll
Against the coral reef;
Ebbing the tide of
Eternity.

William Frank Andrews

UNTITLED

I could not see because my eyes
Were blinded by my fears;
The more I faced the roaring tide
The more my face was seared.

Broad waves around my ship did roar
There was no land in sight;
I prayed but only doubted more –
Until I saw the light.

When Jesus walked out on the sea
I felt my fears subside;
I knew his hand was holding me
Above the roaring tide.

And now by faith I see the light
My heart will hurt no more;
For I have Jesus in my sight
And I will reach the shore!

January 25, 1996

From Humble Beginnings

LITTLE BOY OF COMITAN

When he asked me for the *pesos*
With his little hand stretched out
I withdrew for just a moment
Not knowing what it was about.

As he told in broken English
Little fellow man-to-man
How he came to be a homeless
Little boy of Comitan.

Told how dad had died in prison
How his mom could not be found
So he wandered streets a-begging
Sleeping nightly on the ground.

So I gave him many *pesos*.
Wouldn't you have done the same?
Now my heart is feeling better;
Little boy of Comitan.

April, 2002, Mexico mission trip with Operation Latin America

William Frank Andrews

POLITIKIN'

He came to kiss the baby fair
Or so at least he claims;
What really brings him out this way
Is my 'X' beside his name.

Says he, "This road could use some oil,
Would take away the sludge;
I might could get it done for you
If I were County Judge."

Says I, "This road don't need no oil,
'Cause it don't go nowhere;
The one that leaves this road alone
Deserves the Judge's Chair."

Editor's note: Politikin' was the author's winning entry in the Tennessee Homecoming 1986 Calendar Contest.

Part 2: Franklin

William Frank Andrews

MY HOME TOWN

Take some small-town easy living
And a little civic pride;
Mix 'em up with friendly neighbors
Who are always at your side.

Add a little touch of sunshine
And a little bit of rain;
And lots of shops and candy stores
Sprinkled down on Main.

Old town-houses and the churches
And a statue on the square;
Makes no matter where you wander
You will wish that you were there.

The policeman and the postman
Friendly people who can smile;
Say "Good morning" when you pass 'em,
Glad to go that extra mile.

Where on Earth is such a heaven?
Come along and you will see;
A place that's always kind and friendly
And it's FRANKLIN, TENNESSEE.

August 29, 1985

From Humble Beginnings

DOWNTOWN FRANKLIN

You might take some bricks and mortar
And build yourself some fancy mall;
Add lots of glass and asphalt parking
And some silly name to call.

But never ever this I promise,
In your wildest scheme of things,
Will you find more joy in shopping
Than Downtown Franklin always brings.

You could hire yourself a drummer
And an old-time brass band;
But you'd still be out-of-step
With the best spot in the land.

Downtown Franklin – people, places
All the merchants always fair;
No mall in all its gleam and splendor
Can replace someone who cares.

So if you have a buck to spend
Just make sure it is well-spent;
Bring it all to Downtown Franklin;
That's how our merchants pay the rent.

February 1986

William Frank Andrews

MEETING OF THE WATERS

It had to be chance – this meeting;
This grand lady and I;
She standing so stately and so serene
And I just a passer-by.

She's known as *Meeting of the Waters*
'Cause rivers around her entwine;
For many long years she has stood here
Just getting better with time.

What marvelous stories she tells me
As softly she opens her arms,
And holds me ever-so gently
To whisper softly her charms.

"My hearth has known comfort and heartache
My stairs a small child's delight;
My roof has brought shelter and kindness
For strangers out of the night.

"The Perkins, the Woolwines and Trousdales
And now the Ridley Wills,
Have called me home for the ages
As I stand looking over these hills.

From Humble Beginnings

"My new master has given so much of himself
New plaster, new love and new paint;
I'll hold him close to my bosom today
And someday I'll make him my saint.

"And to you this stranger just passing –
I'm glad you could meet me today!
For now I'm no longer just an old house
But a wonderful home by-the-way."

For Ridley, December 4, 1990

William Frank Andrews

HOMES OF THE MASTER

Far away in my memory a small country church
Where with Grandma I went as a child;
A horse pulled the buggy fast over the road
We laughed and we sang o'er the miles.

Though many a mile I have wandered
Away from the place of my birth;
Nothing today is more precious
To me than this small country church.

A small congregation of people;
A meeting place simple and sure –
Sure beats a big church in the city
If all the hearts are not pure.

Please give me a small country building,
A cemetery right by its side;
With bells ringing out o'er the valley
To help me cross over the tide.

Yes, here let me rest until judgment
Until the last trumpet shall sound;
And let no one judge me in anger
For deeds that I've done they have found.

From Humble Beginnings

OUR MONUMENT

Standing stately in the center
Of the Franklin town square
Looking southward to the glory
Of a land that once was there.

Our monument to vanquished heroes
Valiant dead – the honored men;
Resting now in peaceful meadows
Honored now for courage then.

Let us hope for bright tomorrows –
Let our monument foretell –
A time of peace in all our nation
For we know that "war is hell."

June 14, 1984

William Frank Andrews

MY HOMETOWN BANK

I went down to my hometown bank
To check me out some dough.
The doors were locked; the shades were drawn;
The sign said, "Sorry, closed."

There on the front was the chairman of the board.
I knew I was in luck.
He asked me what I needed.
I said, "A hundred bucks!"

He simply took his wallet out
And in the nick of time;
He asked me if I needed more.
I said no this is fine.

He never asked my history;
No forms; no note to sign.
You see my hometown banker is
A special friend of mine.

So the next time you pass the Franklin Square
And Gordon is there on the street;
The bank may be closed but that's OK;
He'll make a loan that's neat!

From Humble Beginnings

Now I've been around for a long, long time.
I've had my ups and downs;
But Franklin National on the square
Is the bank of my hometown.

May 1991

William Frank Andrews

FASHION CLEANERS

If all your clothes are dirty;
And it doesn't seem quite fair,
I have a word to tell you
That will keep you from despair.

For you I have a friend to see
On Seventh Avenue;
There they take your dirty clothes
And make them look like new.

A smile from Dot when you come in;
With arms stuffed full of work –
And Mrs. Duke that gracious lady;
Her duty will not shirk.

And if you have to wait a bit
Your time won't be a flop;
'Cause you can read the morning news
It's always there on top.

I like to smell the sunshine;
My clothes as fresh as May,
This you get at Fashion Cleaners
Each and every day.

From Humble Beginnings

So if your clothes are looking shabby,
This I recommend – you guessed!
Just take them down to FASHION CLEANERS
For it's there they can get pressed!

Especially for my friends at Fashion Cleaners, January 5, 1986

William Frank Andrews

LORI'S BOOK STORE

Sometimes when I'm not so busy
And I have some idle time;
I like to stroll downtown to Lori's
'Cause it makes me feel just fine.

Books and cards and magazines
And a thousand things or more,
All waiting from an eager perch
Just inside of Lori's store.

Hardy Boys and other mysteries
And the latest from the list;
All the books you ever wanted
And the ones you thought you'd missed.

If you don't have all the knowledge
And you crave a little more;
You can find it down on Fourth
Right in Lori's little store.

So if you have an idle moment
Please make sure it is well spent.
Just don't forget to buy a book
'Cause that's how Lori pays the rent.

August 29, 1985

From Humble Beginnings

LAZY SUMMER

Back when candy was a nickel
Big RC for just a dime,
All the groceries in your basket
Fifteen dollars every time.

Times when friends could get together –
While away the hours of time;
Just by swapping simple stories
Didn't cost a single dime.

How I long for lazy summers
Skinny dipping in the creek;
Fetching fodder from the corn row
Good fresh food for cows to eat.

Grabbling 'taters in the garden
In the early part of June;
Smell of lilacs fresh as morning
With their smell of sweet perfume.

Chop tobacco – hoe the corn row;
Weeds the rain has made to grow –
Higher than the little fellow
Who is working with the hoe.

William Frank Andrews

How I long for harvest moonlight,
Work is done, crops in the barn.
Time to cut the wood for winter –
Time to spin another yarn.

From Humble Beginnings

JUST LIKE YESTERDAY

Back when candy was a nickel
Big RC for just a dime
The local hardware store was waiting
Just to go and spend some time.

Everything you ever wanted
Plows and rope and things that shine;
Even had a keg of nails
Where you could sit and spin a line.

Almost every Saturday morning
Would find me in the hardware store.
Nuts and bolts and belts and harness
And a thousand items more.

Now I know that times are changin'
In a silly sort of way
But I know where I can go now
And it's just like yesterday.

S.E. Farnsworth down on Margin
When you go you're bound to say,
"Goodness sakes I've finally found it,
And it's just like yesterday."

William Frank Andrews

You'll always find the doors are open;
And the smile from Ned will say,
"Thanks a lot for stopping by,
We treat you just like yesterday."

From Humble Beginnings

THE PEPPER PATCH

Down-home goodness always cooking
From down in Franklin, Tennessee.
The Pepper Patch is making goodies
From their old-time factory.

Dot Smith and all her angels
Working hard both night and day;
This catalogue will help discover
All the things we'll send your way.

Tipsy cake and Pepper Jelly
Made just like down on the farm;
All the herbs and all the spices
Bottled up with lots of charm.

So if you have a friend or two
Who just don't like to cook;
Just order straight from The Pepper Patch.
You'll find it all here in our book.

For The Pepper Patch catalogue, November 28, 1984

William Frank Andrews

DEATH OF A GREAT HOUSE

All that remains are two mighty timbers
Of a house once noble and grand;
A plantation house; magnificence bold
But now they are mining the land.

Phosphate the mineral destroying our land
And bringing our history to dust;
It seems to me one acre they'd spare
And leave us some memories in trust.

I'm haunted in dreams by a house that has died –
For want of a fortune in gold.
Now nothing remains but holes in the land
While miners have money to hold.

Whenever I pass this barren landscape
A picture comes back for a while;
Of a charming old house with chimneys so tall
Where once I played as a child.

Somehow I must stand up and be heard
Before all our treasures are gone.
The death of a house as noble as this
Must not pass alone and unknown.

August 25, 1984

From Humble Beginnings

I cried the day I passed the Walters House where I lived with my grandparents in the mid 1950s. The huge corner posts were lying on the ground in agony where they once pointed toward the sky, holding up a grand house built just prior to the War Between the States by the Walters family.

Part 3: Hometown People

William Frank Andrews

FOR 'PEK' GUNN AT EIGHTY

I have a friend with silver hair and lines upon his face;
A poet in his native land; a simple man with grace.
From humble earth God made this man eighty years ago,
To bring to us some lasting song; a song of mirth – a poet.

From Tumbling Creek back in the hills to national renown
'Pek' Gunn has given joy to all the villages and towns.
There'll never be another man whose pen will sing such
words;
The poems he writes for simple folk will evermore be heard.

Our state has honored Mr. Gunn as poet laureate;
And when he leaves this world of toil no one will soon forget.
So here's to you my good friend 'Pek' I hope I'm honored so.
Would you please pass your mantle on to me if you should
go?

Some kindred I must claim to you for I'm a poet too.
Someday I trust that I shall be a poet just like you.
So 'Pek' keep writing lots of verse and put it down for fate
I hope you have a hundred years and then we'll celebrate!

*From Frank Andrews on your 80th birthday, and from your friend
Brent Andrews*

From Humble Beginnings

FRANK LYNCH – MY HERO

I only can spare you a moment old man;
To sit and listen to you;
So come if you can in the time that we have
And tell me a story or two.

Tell me some stories of love and of war;
The story of coming back home.
Tell of the moonlight on waters so blue;
Your promise to nevermore roam.

Frank Lynch was a soldier in a long ago war.
Now he is stooped with age;
But as a young boy of only eighteen
He stood on a faraway stage.

That stage was a war in a faraway land.
That hell was not his by choice.
He was called by his country to the roar of the gun.
Without anger he answered the voice.

Frank Lynch you're a hero I give you my word;
I shall never forget what you gave;
And if I remain on the earth when you're gone
I'll plant a white cross on your grave.

For my new friend Frank Lynch, October 6, 2002

William Frank Andrews

MY TRIBUTE TO MISS EULALIE JEFFERSON

If I could go back to childhood again
With all the plans that I made;
I'd like to start in Miss Jefferson's room –
My teacher in second grade.

Although I'm grown up and a grandfather now;
Miss Jefferson is older than me;
I want to go back and sit by her side;
And let her explain to me.

How could she love me when I was so poor?
And most times I needed a bath;
But she never made any difference with me
Or anyone else in the class.

I do not know what the future may hold;
But one thing makes me so glad;
For all the good Miss Jefferson taught
I know I can never be bad.

Miss Jefferson lives in a house downtown;
An old house cozy and snug;
And every time I pass that way
I stop and give her a hug.

From Humble Beginnings

She lives next door to my children now –
And grandchildren – how lucky they are;
I remind them so often they know very well
They're living next door to a star.

With love and devotion, Frank Andrews, your second-grade student (1946)

William Frank Andrews

TO AMY AND DAVID

Just a simple country wedding
Where our vows we say for life.
I David Dean do take thee Amy
For to be my loving wife.

And I, Amy take thee David
Strong as mountains of your birth
Unto thee I give this promise:
I'll be yours for good or worse.

All my life has been so empty –
Now my search is finally o'er;
In your arms I find my heaven;
I will leave you nevermore.

Now our lives – all hope and promise
Shall forever be as one;
With each other we'll be happy
As we share the rising sun.

To our friends who came to see us
In our mountaintop serene,
May God bless you as you watch us;
Greatest love you've ever seen.

With sincere love and best wishes from your friends Frank and Carolyn Andrews

From Humble Beginnings

RCT. SCOTT A BURCHYETT – SOON TO BE A U.S. MARINE

I want to go back to my Tennessee hills;
Back to my Tennessee girl;
Back to my church – my mother and dad
Back to my Tennessee world.

But tomorrow I 'wake before daybreak
To the sound of "left, left" and "right."
I'll give 'em my sweat and maybe my tears
'Til day turns again into night.

Whenever it seems I can take it no more;
I'll keep drawing strength from within.
In such a short time I'll pass through this hour
And join the ranks of the men.

So tell all my friends whenever they ask,
Scott Burchyett is doing just fine;
In spite of the heat and in spite of the rain,
I'm leading the pack from behind.

The next time you see me – I promise you true;
This me you never have seen.
The young man who left you with fear in his heart
Is now a U.S. Marine!

William Frank Andrews

ANNA CLAIRE SMITHSON

Anna Claire Smithson we bid farewell
The hymns they sing are true.
And when the last sad note is heard
We'll still be missing you!

Your life was such a bouquet
And your treasures sent ahead
Now wait for you in Heaven,
For this the Master said.

Your life on earth is ended,
Your long sojourn is o'er.
God rest your soul in Heaven,
Until we join once more.

Written at the funeral of Miss Claire, December 15, 1984

From Humble Beginnings

SISTER JEAN

I am Jean – my brother's sister.
I have been a strong oak tree.
Now the time has come to leave you;
No more you'll shelter under me.

To my beloved husband Buck
I have loved you 'til the last;
You have been my strength – my tower;
Though the storms did cross our path.

You have given all within you –
You were mine until the end;
Although I'm gone you must remember;
You were always my best friend.

And to my son who always charmed me;
With your witty little ways;
Now your memories give you comfort
'Til the ending of your days.

To my friends and all my family;
Those of you who came today;
Don't weep for me but just remember
Soon you too must come this way.

William Frank Andrews

TO MARY ANN AT FORTY

I know a special lady
The sister of my wife;
This lady just turned forty;
She's used up half her life.

This lady is a teacher
And don't you just forget;
If not for her big sister,
This girl could be my pet.

In all her years of living
Her charmed and special life
She's been a wondrous mother
And a very special wife.

Two very special children
Melinda and sweet John
Have made her life worth living,
We're glad that they could come.

So here's to you my sister Ann
Tonight when you're in bed,
I really am quite sorry
That all you got was RED!

With love and devotion from your brother-in-law

From Humble Beginnings

MY SISTER'S HOUSE

Have you ever been to the village of Fly
On a lazy summer day;
And sat by the creek while the children played,
And rocked all your troubles away?

Well I know a place just over the hill,
Across from an old country store,
Where love doth abide for all who come by
To sit for an hour or more.

There's an old country house at the side of the road;
And Sister will open her arms
To share all she has in perfect delight;
Her love; her family; her charms.

So if ever you happen by chance on your course
And the last of the corners go 'round;
You'll find her there just waiting for you
Right in the heart of downtown.

To Andy from your brother-in-law

William Frank Andrews

MY TRIBUTE TO DANNY DUKE

There's the pulpit standing empty
It is Sunday – church-time hour
And the voice that used to lead us
Is singing now in Heaven's choir.

We will miss you Brother Danny
Faithful Christian; loving dad.
And remember with our sorrow
All the good times that we had.

Now we praise our loving Savior
He who watches from above;
You are resting now in Heaven
In his wondrous arms of love.

Now your songbook lying idle;
It is resting for a while.
You have used it for God's service,
Since you were a little child.

Yes we miss you Brother Danny
And we seem so all alone;
But we'll join you some tomorrow
In that glorious heavenly home.

From Humble Beginnings

A TRIBUTE TO HAYWOOD COLE

I looked into a crystal ball
The future to behold,
But the things I saw were about the past,
Of a man named Haywood Cole.

This man first came upon the scene
Nigh sixty years ago.
He stood up tall and there exclaimed,
"A-teaching I will go!"

I see him as he made his choice;
And then prepared to be
The greatest teacher Grassland School
Could ever hope to see.

Now after thirty years or more
He's gonna get his wish;
He's going to the riverbank,
To educate the fish.

Now I don't know if fish can talk
Or learn to read and write;
If not – when Cole throws them the bait
They'd better get out of sight.

William Frank Andrews

Now we are searching high and low
We'll look at every face
In vain, we know 'cause Haywood Cole
Could never be replaced.

From Humble Beginnings

TO DONALD PIERCE AT FIFTY

Please make something clear to me
Donald Pierce sir-ree.
How does it feel to be so old
A half a century?

And you say, "Why I'm not so old –
Don't feel it anyway.
You're not too old unless you dread
The coming of the day.

"I'm always up before the sun
For others good to do.
I'll mind your kids and run your chores
And bring some news to you.

"All my years I've been a friend,
To you and all mankind.
I know when life down here is o'er
A better home I'll find.

"So if you think that fifty's old,
Please let me re-impart:
Some folks are old at twenty-one,
But I'm still young at heart.

William Frank Andrews

TO DONALD H. PIERCE DEPARTED LOVED ONE

Sadness now surrounds our presence,
As we weep for our friend Don.
All our hearts are numb with sorrow
As his life we look upon.

Not so old in years he gave us,
Though so worn from many miles,
Service always there for others;
And he did it with a smile.

Many years devoted husband
And a father who was proud.
All of us who really knew him
Now can sing his praises loud.

His life was service to his Master,
Who now has him in his care;
Let us rejoice as Christian brethren
And prepare to meet him there.

What reward that now awaits you
Donald Pierce beloved friend.
We release you to the Master
Who is with you 'til the end.

From Humble Beginnings

Though it's hard to be without you
And we weep with broken heart.
We will soon be joined together
There we nevermore shall part.

Though your life on Earth is ended
And you now must cross the tide
With God you stand and wait to join us
Over on the other side.

A special friend

William Frank Andrews

FOR MOM – MY SPECIAL MOTHER-IN-LAW

I know a special lady,
The mother of my wife
I call her Mom 'cause she's so dear
A bright spot in my life.

Next Sunday is the day we honor
The moms-in-law so fair;
And I've got one so special
I'll write a line to share.

In all the years I've known her
No unkind words I've heard.
She's always there to courage give
And offer kinder words.

When I was young and courting
Her oldest daughter fair;
No one could feel as welcome
As I when I was there.

Sunday dinners – something special
Good food and cold iced tea;
Back then I felt that every meal
She cooked them just for me.

From Humble Beginnings

Next summer will be silver
For your oldest child and me;
And Mom my thanks to you I give
For sharing her with me.

I know not what the years may bring
What troubles; what travail;
But Mom I know I'll count on you.
Your love for me won't fail.

Mother-in-law day, 1983

William Frank Andrews

TO JIMMY SMITHSON AT FORTY - 1988

I now have decided after so many years
That nothing in life is much fun.
My working and striving for all of these years,
Won't buy me a place in the sun.

Now forty long years have crept up on me.
They've wiped the smile from my face.
I'm over the hill in so many ways.
I think I'm losing the race.

For so many things I'm thankful,
My God; my children; my wife.
I've tried very hard a foundation to build
For God the rest of my life.

It goes without saying – not much money I bring;
My pockets are empty and bare;
And sometimes I think my daddy's purse strings
Are hanging too high in the air.

But I've always been the family's pride;
And loving's been easy to get;
So stick with me for forty more years.
'Cause you ain't seen nothing yet!

Happy Birthday from your brother-in-law

From Humble Beginnings

BRIAN

'Tis night and time to go to bed
But Brian is still awake.
What little things a boy will do
What excuses they will make!

Though supper was had two hours ago,
"I'm hungry still," he says.
"Just one more drink of milk for me
Before I go to bed."

Brian is five and that's the age
When sleep just seems to flee.
I think I'll make it to Dream Land,
Resting on mother's knee.

'Tis night and time to go to bed
And Brian is fast asleep.
He finally knelt to say his prayers
I pray the Lord his soul will keep.

William Frank Andrews

STEPHANIE

Stephanie is her daddy's daughter
With long blonde curls and tresses;
Eager for life's adventures
In dainty gowns and dresses.

When she grows up she'll be a queen
A palace with ladies in waiting;
'Til then she'll have to bide her time
With books and games and waiting.

Time slips away so swiftly it seems
And suddenly it is tomorrow;
And Stephanie is all grown up
Never a friend to sorrow.

From Humble Beginnings

PUSHER TRAINS (COWAN, TENNESSEE)

Cowan the city of pusher trains;
McKnight sits on the ground;
Watching the pushers at work all day
Chugging and pushing around.

McKnight is now near eighty-five
He chats with passers-by.
Talk of yesteryear, and trains,
A gleam is in his eye.

Cowan is asleep for now –
Shops are closed for good.
McKnight still hopes for better days;
Like yesterday – I wish they could.

The pusher is a special train;
More power can be found,
To push the freight up o'er the hill
And make that southern town.

I know the day will come again
When trains will have their day,
But ole McKnight won't be around
To sit and have his say.

William Frank Andrews

The mountain steel – the tunnel dark
Waits up the hill away –
The pusher train will help us all
To have a better day.

From Humble Beginnings

THE SHRINER

I'm proud to be a Shriner
In the land of the brave and the free.
America is my homeland –
My state is Tennessee.

I'll proudly march to the beat of a drum
And hold Old Glory high.
My heart forever shall esteem
This flag that's passing by.

For many brave people in war and death
Have shed their blood for me;
And I today can now be proud
They gave their lives for me.

So come with us to our next parade
And march along with me.
We need each other more each day
To keep America free.

November 15, 1988

William Frank Andrews

CLARENCE JOHNSON

Clarence Johnson, my old friend;
I'm sorry you are sick;
But I'll still beat you playing golf
Without my brand-new stick!

Please take comfort with the thought –
And it is such a shame;
I'm out hitting tons of balls
And sharpening up my game.

So here's to you my friend C.J.
Please hurry and get well!
'Cause you might have a prospect
That I will try to sell.

Your forever friend, June 17, 1986

From Humble Beginnings

NOBLE CARSON, 1905 - 1990

Once in a while in the annals of time
A good man comes along;
Just working and praying and doing his best
To fill the world with song.

Faithful to family – faithful to God
Not seeking himself to acclaim;
One person we've known this description will fit
He's Noble Carson by name.

He came on the scene in Nineteen-O-Five,
Such humble beginnings he knew;
And for all of his life the heritage he built
Was strong and brave and true.

I know there are men who never fit in;
They never make their mark.
They live their lives in search of fame
And wind up in the dark.

But Noble Carson made his mark.
He caused the world to smile.
And now the Lord has called him home
To rest for a little while.

William Frank Andrews

Though the world has lost a flower
That can never be replaced;
When all the stars come out tonight
You'll see his smiling face.

Especially for his children Montelle, Ruth, Ray, Joe and Witsie and all the grandchildren, December 1990

From Humble Beginnings

SUMMER

Summer, you can always charm me
With your darling little curls.
What a darling little lady,
What a sweet and precious girl.

Now that you are getting older
And real soon you're turning eight,
I must give a simple warning
Just to try to keep you straight.

Watch yourself and do not falter.
Little boys will seek your charm.
You must take some good advice –
Turn them down will do no harm.

Hazel eyes and ruby lips
Do not make a good disguise
For a sweet and charming lady
Please remember my advice.

Always keep your wits about you
Remember God is on your side
And you'll grow up very pretty
And you'll always bring us pride.

Part 4: Trades

William Frank Andrews

THE PLUMBER

On the coldest day of winter
Frozen pipes about to bust
Got to find myself a plumber
Someone I can really trust.

Find the phone book yellow pages
"Fingers walking" all the way.
There he is among the others,
With his smiling little face.

"Can you come now?" words I ask him
In exasperated tones.
Pipes a-bustin' at the seams now,
So I said, "Well please come on!"

Hours later work is over
Water running smooth and free –
And the bill that he presents me
Scares the stuffing out of me.

Then I ask how can he do it –
Demand such prices; so it goes.
"For the job you pay so little.
You pay for mostly what I knows."

From Humble Beginnings

THE VEGETABLE MAN

The familiar sounds of steel-shod hooves;
Ring on ancient cobblestones –
Man of the vegetable cart
Behind a tired nag.

The clip-clop of tired feet plod homeward
To rest for tomorrow's dawn,
Fresh fruits and vegetables
And another day.

William Frank Andrews

PAINTERS

The painters came today
And splashed and sprayed
New colors on my walls.

Do you suppose they stay long enough
To clean the paint from the windows
So the sun can see in again?

So I can see out?

From Humble Beginnings

THE SECRETARY

The wheels of commerce could not turn
Without her smiling face.
And when she's out there is no one
To ever take her place.

When ill winds chance to blow her way
And trials leave her low;
She smiles right through the toughest spot
And no one ever knows.

The boss is in – he's fast asleep.
Don't tell it – he would die!
So if you call while he's asleep
Again she has to lie.

She's such an inspiration to
All who come in touch;
Her work is never done it seems;
Her pay not half enough.

So here's to you sweet secretary
We honor you today!
We hope you'll stick around a while
Until you're better paid.

April 25, 1990

William Frank Andrews

THE FARMER'S PLIGHT

Said the farmer to his neighbor,
As he stood across the fence,
"The price of land is getting higher
And to me it makes no sense.

"I can't take it any longer
So I guess I'm selling out.
Cows and pigs don't make much money
Price of corn is down no doubt.

"My father's father came before him
Settled where the soil was deep;
And we've kept it all together
As the best that we could keep.

"Now they're talking 'bout a factory
That is coming down the road;
And the land that's all around me
Now is gone; it's all been sold.

"And our sleepy little village
Waking up like places bold;
I've got money in my pocket
But the Devil's got my soul."

August 5, 1985

From Humble Beginnings

THE LEADER

Out in every kind of weather
Late at night though hot or cold
Chasing all the leads that give you
Stories for the type so bold.

Down the street comes Bailey Leopard
Fighting for a new deadline –
Got to get one final story
To the printer just in time.

Here's a man with all the courage –
Print the news the way it is;
Never cover up a story
Just because of who it is.

Small town paper – you're a star;
Williamson County's one alone,
The LEADER is my favorite paper
'Cause it is so down-home owned.

All the advertising dollars
Spent at home will help to pay
For the things we all enjoy
Each and every blessed day.

William Frank Andrews

Ten years old and celebratin'
The LEADER is so young and strong!
Franklin's only home-town paper
Make it now your very own!

On the 10th Anniversary of the Williamson Leader, *August 1983*

From Humble Beginnings

THE REALTOR

A Realtor's life is never easy;
With a client working late.
While you look at seven houses
I can't remember when I ate.

A house for you – someplace to live
To me it's food to eat.
Gotta sell a lot of houses
Keeping shoes on my kids' feet.

Honest always this I promise
Never cover up the bad;
I will work from dawn to dark
Best friend you ever had.

Days and weeks we'll keep on looking
'Til we find the very best.
Now you offer half the value
Somehow you'll have to give the rest.

Seller's mad for such an offer –
Says you're crazy – I agree.
But I have to keep on smiling
So you'll keep on trusting me.

William Frank Andrews

All the effort finally over
Closing day will be so smooth.
All the nerves that once were shattered;
Buyers – Sellers now can move.

A Realtor's life is never easy;
Hours long and work is hard;
But somehow it all seems worth it
With my SOLD sign in your yard.

From Humble Beginnings

ALL AS ONE

I choose to be a Realtor
To make my livelihood;
I accept the responsibility
To make my business good.

I do not stand alone today.
My voice will now be loud.
I join the ranks of many more;
Of them I can be proud.

From every town and village
Throughout the U.S.A.,
My brothers and my sisters
All stand with me today.

So if your load is heavy,
And you think it can't be done;
Just call upon your Realtor friend
For we are all as one!

December 15, 1988

William Frank Andrews

THE CARPENTER

Now I can't wash the clothes I wear
Nor cook the things I eat;
But I can build a home for you
And make it look so neat.

To learn my craft I spent the years,
Learned much by trial and error;
So everything seems easier now
To put it all together.

All day long I work with wood.
I saw and nail and bind.
But when the day is finally done
I'm further still behind.

When I shall die and leave this earth
My monument shall be –
The homes I built and left behind
For those left here to see.

My trade I love – to build is fun.
I hope I pass the grade.
For this most noble, honored craft
Was also Jesus' trade.

*For my father-in-law, Walter Lee Smithson, whom I have come to love
as a father*

Above, Grandmother Mona Sullivan pictured circa 1949 in front of the Williamson County sharecropper's shack where she lived with her family. Sullivan raised 13 children and two grandchildren, including the author. Below, Frank Andrews (at left) is pictured with his future wife, Carolyn Smithson, and her younger brother Jimmy outside the Gospel Lighthouse Pentecostal Church in Franklin, Tennessee, where Jimmy is now pastor.

Above, Frank Andrews and his older sister Jean on the farm in 1946, and below, Frank poses with the family bicycle at 9 years old.

Above, Frank and Carolyn Andrews pictured at their June 1959 wedding. Below, Frank is pictured as a private in the U.S. Army Medical Corps. The army photo was taken in San Antonio, Texas, in December 1961.

Above, Andrews paused for a picture at his army post in Ft. Carson, Colorado, in 1962 after hearing that his first son Victor had been born back home in Tennessee. Below, the Andrews family is pictured in 1991 (left to right: Brent, Carolyn, Frank, Becky, and Victor).

Part 5: "My wife, my children, my world."

William Frank Andrews

CAROLYN (1956)

The cold still silence of the night
Brings back a memory.
It also gives a thrill of heart
To a girl and boy like me.

There is no thrill like the kiss of her lips
Or smile of sweet embrace,
That a boy in wonder thinks about
When he sees her smiling face.

No daring exploit of bravery
Or daring dashing ride
Could ever give such a thrill of heart
As she can when she's by my side.

I can forget the cares of life
And for one moment be
Like some most noble wealthy king
When she is here with me.

From Humble Beginnings

TWEEDLE-DEE-DEE

Tweedle-dee Tweedle-dee Tweedle-dee-dum
Howbeit that you so lately have come –
Down by the old mill searching for me,
Tweedle-dee Tweedle-dee Tweedle-dee-dee.

Where are you going with spring in your step?
Why here of late have our date you not kept?
When will I be safe to say, "Please marry me"?
Tweedle-dee Tweedle-dee Tweedle-dee-dee.

When will your vain promise come to an end?
Where could you start if your ways you would mend?
Keep up your gait and some bad end you'll see.
Tweedle-dee Tweedle-dee Tweedle-dee-dee.

First you told Johnny and next you told Bill –
That they you would marry and give 'em a thrill.
Now after much wooing you have promised me
Tweedle-dee Tweedle-dee Tweedle-dee-dee.

I'll make you so happy for the rest of your life.
You'll never be sorry that you are my wife.
If we cling together, soon there'll be three –
Tweedle-dee Tweedle-dee Tweedle-dee-dee.

William Frank Andrews

LOVERS

At dawn I stood alone and cried
Of dreams that were untrue.
I pledged to die before I'd give
Up dreams of loving you.

I wandered through the day half-lost;
My mind was still on you.
And when you called me on the phone
I felt not half so blue.

Down the lane we strolled that night.
You seemed so all alone.
I wondered how to touch your heart
And make your love my own.

Cold was the night though the wind stood still.
The moon played its game on your face.
The heart knows when it's free to love,
And when it can interlace.

From Humble Beginnings

TO A FARAWAY LOVE

The mountain rises 'neath my feet
To touch the sky above.
To stand up high is bittersweet
Without someone you love.

Not long ago I touched the sky
With love and happiness.
But like the leaf that soon must die
I'll die of loneliness.

While all the world shall sleep tonight
I'll climb this mountain tall,
And while the stars shall make their flight
To you my love I'll call.

William Frank Andrews

KING FOR A DAY

Make me your king for a day my love.
Tell me you'll be my queen.
Take me to places that I haven't been –
To places that I haven't seen.

Come wander with me through meadows unknown.
Come rest with me by the way.
We'll take a trip through the tunnel of love.
Make me your king for a day.

I'll always believe in somethings good;
In all things honest and true.
Now more than ever in all of my life
I really believe in you.

If I could be wiser than all kings of old;
And only those wise things say;
My life would know true happiness
If I were your king for a day.

From Humble Beginnings

TWENTY-ONE YEARS

A beach in the emerald isles
A time for celebration –
Married twenty-one years to the woman I love.
What joy and jubilation!

Room two-seventeen the Ambassador Beach;
We loved and started all over.
With mem'ries of love and joys we shared
In songs and fields of clover.

Please say it again, "I love you my dear,"
Words that I've heard before.
I'll give you myself the rest of my life –
And hope for twenty-one more.

In the Bahamas, 1980

William Frank Andrews

TWENTY-FIVE YEARS

Suddenly all my years of marriage
Now add up to twenty-five —
Silver year we celebrate you
The twelfth of June it's twenty-five.

Martha all these years I've loved you;
Your hair reflects the silver, too;
I could never ever tell you
All the love I have for you!

"Martha" is the name I've given
My special name to tell you true
How my heart has always loved you
All my life has been for you.

What a mother, wife and lover
You have been for me these years;
You have made my world much brighter
You have shared my joy and tears.

Now we wait for glad tomorrows,
And we'll have some sorrows too —
But my steps will be more steady
If I have the love of you.

From Humble Beginnings

Looking back on our sweet union
To the year of Fifty-Nine –
Sickness; health and richer-poorer
Until death I know you're mine.

Silver anniversary June 12, 1984

William Frank Andrews

'MARTHA'

Martha you can always charm me
Take from me things that please;
All my money love and kisses
Given to you on my knees.

I have loved you for so long now
I can't picture life alone.
When we loved as little children
We wished then that we were grown.

All my vows today I give you
Renewed again with simple grace
Never ever will I leave you
And the splendor of your face.

Many treasures you have brought me
Many pleasures we have known.
All our lives we'll spend together
Lovely times from seed we've sown.

Martha little-pet I named you
Name I gave some time ago;
Just to let you know I love you,
And to let the whole world know.

From Humble Beginnings

LOVE SONG TO MARTHA

Martha, I can see you're getting older
By the silver in your hair
By the way you smile and touch me
By the way you rock your chair.

Soon we'll see another summer
We'll look back across the years;
At the joys we've shared together,
All the happiness and tears.

I remember it was summer
In the year of Fifty-Nine
When we pledged our love forever
And today it's still just fine.

I'm so thankful for you Martha,
For the love that we have known;
For the years we've spent together;
For the tenderness you've shown.

Now I don't know about the future
Only God can understand.
But I reassure you, Martha
That I'll always be your man.

May 12, 2004

William Frank Andrews

HOMES OF MY HEART

These are the homes of my family
Since first I married my wife;
Where love that we shared in splendor
Has given our children their lives.

First on the list the apartment
Two rooms and sharing a bath;
Love was so strong we never would mind
If we only had a path!

Next came our cottage so humble,
In the woods this house very small
We sold it with hearts that were broken
When Uncle Sam gave us his call.

A number of homes have come later
And *Thornhill* we're missing you so;
But never again am I moving.
From here to Mt. Hope I will go.

All of our homes have been heaven,
Since June Nineteen Fifty-Nine;
And Martha and all of my children
Have really made it just fine.

From Humble Beginnings

MY SHIP

There's a hill of green behind my house;
A hill with trees sublime.
Although this hill belongs not to me
Sometimes I pretend it's mine.

I like to pretend this hill is a ship,
The captain of this ship is me.
With wind in my sails and anchors aweigh
I sail away out to sea.

At times when life's little troubles
Have a way of getting me down;
I go to my hill and sail far away
Where troubles can never be found.

William Frank Andrews

MY CHILDREN

I can hear the muffled chatter
Of my children as they play;
And my garden makes then welcome
Where they're safe with me today.

When I think about tomorrow –
When they've grown a bit and gone;
And such thinking overwhelms me
For it's then I'll be alone.

Then my mind is made to settle
On my God from up above;
He will keep them warm and sheltered
In his arms so full of love.

From Humble Beginnings

TO VICTOR ON YOUR LEAVING FOR COLLEGE (AUG. 19, 1981)

I was going through your things today
Some things you left behind.
And as I did your nineteen years
Came drifting through my mind.

You came to us in Sixty-Two,
When fall was in the air.
Your love has blessed us every day
You are a son so fair.

We've found your books and magazines
All stacked and neatly stored.
You used to aggravate us some
With all the things you'd hoard.

Then there's your bed and chest of drawers
Your mother picked for you,
So when you marry and move again
You'll come and take those, too.

You've left in us an empty place
That only you can fill.
And when you can come home again
You'll give our hearts a thrill.

William Frank Andrews

TO VICTOR AND SUZANNE ON YOUR WEDDING (JUNE 23, 1990)

I stood there by the window
As I watched you catch the bus;
You seemed so very small to leave me
But I knew somehow you must.

And everything turned out OK,
At school for you that day;
'Even said you loved your teacher –
And she took you out to play.

All these years I've been your father;
And I've tried to do my best;
To take away the storms of life
And to help you pass the test.

Now I know I need not tell you –
You can see I'm very proud;
For you have grown to be a man
And to me you brought no clouds.

Five years now my business partner –
Father – Son, no angry word;
I thank you for the inspiration
And the compliments I've heard.

From Humble Beginnings

As I stand here in the chapel
And I watch you take a wife;
You seem so very big and strong
For this adventure in your life.

But as you leave me Victor now
Just a word from me to you;
Love this girl as I loved your mom
And to her always be true.

For if I had made the choice for you
Though I can't – for you're a man;
My choice for you would be the same
As your loving sweet Suzanne.

Love Daddy

William Frank Andrews

A FARM AT THE END OF THE ROAD

Sometimes when I'm weary at ending of day,
And my soul just wants to lie down,
I go to my farm at the end of the road,
Where peace and sweet rest can be found.

My wife and four children are waiting for me,
On my spread that I call *Road's End Farm*;
There I pray to my God at starting of day;
That he'll always keep us from harm.

Each morning I wake with a challenge to face;
Each day is a heavier load;
But I know in my heart at ending of day,
There's my farm at the end of the road.

Someday when my life shall lose all its charm,
And I move to my Heavenly abode
I ask you dear Lord to make for me there,
A farm at the end of the road.

Lovingly written for Victor and family springtime 2004

From Humble Beginnings

WILLIAM PATRICK ANDREWS
(DEDICATION SUNDAY, JAN. 5, 1992)

Dear Will,
Special days and special moments
William Patrick little child.
Today we give you back to Jesus,
For He's the One who gave you life.

You were born to loving parents;
They will teach you right from wrong;
Teach you how to read your Bible –
Teach you how to sing a song.

When you grow a little older
And you meet the world outside,
You'll be safe 'cause God has promised
That He'll always be your guide.

Your roots are deep in Christian heritage;
But you alone must make your choice.
Today this special dedication
Is to make *our* hearts rejoice.

Sometimes darkness may surround you
And the storms may hide the sky;
But remember God is with you
And He's walking by your side.

William Frank Andrews

HANNAH MURIEL ANDREWS (DEDICATION SUNDAY, DEC. 4, 1994)

Dear Hannah,
I've been thinking so much lately
'Bout the things that God has done;
All about a grand-new baby
He has given to my son.

Hannah you will fit this family,
You will fill a special place;
And we welcome you this morning
With your smiling little face.

Now Will can have a little sister;
Mom can have a special girl;
Dad can know the joy and gladness
That you bring into this world.

Little girls are something special
Sent from God with hearts so true;
And Hannah you will always cheer us
When the world would make us blue.

Today we dedicate to Jesus
One bright shining little dear
Hannah Muriel Andrews, darling
We're so very glad you're here!

From Humble Beginnings

WELCOME CLAIRE SUSANNAH ANDREWS (BORN MAY 31, 1997)

Late in May and almost summer,
With the flowers all unfurled;
God sent to us a blessed wonder –
A lovely child; a little girl.

Now we have a brand-new daughter;
And her name is baby Claire.
Just a little bit of dimple –
Just a little bit of hair.

So we dedicate this moment,
Claire Susannah to the Lord.
And we know that he will keep her;
For he promised in his word.

So here I am your special darling;
Hold me closely to your heart.
Promise me through all my ages,
That our love will never part.

Someday in a bright tomorrow,
I'll teach my child a song of you.
Two good parents loving Jesus,
Taught me to him to be true.

William Frank Andrews

CAMPBELL JAMES ANDREWS (DEDICATION FEB. 24, 2002)

Your eyes are as blue as the blue in the sky
Your face is a picture of love.
We dedicate you now in the name of the One
Who sent you from Heaven above.

Your brother and sisters are all standing by
And mother and daddy are proud.
We give you to Jesus forever to keep.
Our hearts are all singing out loud.

You may be the last of the line for me,
So old Poppy will watch you and pray
The name that I gave you – you will carry with pride
Your daddy will show you the way.

So Campbell James our hearts are glad
We love you – one and all.
We give you back to Jesus now
To keep until he calls.

From Humble Beginnings

BETH AT TWENTY MONTHS

Child of my heart how is it that I love you so?
You with your rag-tag doll and smile that I've come to know.
It can't be big brother's britches or mustard in your hair
That causes me to love you so and makes your mommy care.
Is it the way you climb the stairs or jump in bed at night?
Or talk upon the telephone with small child-like delight?
I know your mother loves you too and just as much as me,
But after all the chase you give it's more than I can see:
It's down the stairs – out the doors – cross the street again
But neighbors always bring you back so much to our chagrin.
Is it the way you romp on me when I am tired and weary?
Or bring me back to life again when everything seems dreary?
Perhaps it's just your ripe old age 'cause now you're almost
two.
Whatever be the cause for it I'll give my love to you.
And then when you grow up to be some other fellow's girl,
Just promise me you'll always share with me your little world.

William Frank Andrews

BETH

I think I like to hear the wind that blows
To me; I'm Beth and me nobody knows –
But I shall be as strong as some oak tree;
Someday someone will shelter under me.

I think that I am one not faint of heart.
Somehow these words to you I must impart.
I'm like a river running quiet and still.
I know I'll find a way to climb this hill.

I'll make my way tho' darkness be my path.
No one can take my breath tho' it's my last.
Altho' sometimes the darkness covers me;
I shall be strong so just you wait and see.

Sometimes in vain I try to seek the truth;
And realize that hope is for the youth.
I've come to know this is the life I chose –
But I am Beth and me nobody knows.

From Humble Beginnings

BECKY

I watched you as you slept last night
My little girl of three;
I prayed that I could teach you right;
You mean so much to me.

You're BECKY and your eyes are brown;
You romp the whole day through.
You always smile; you never frown,
Your love is always true.

I watched you as you played today;
Be careful as you go!
I hope your feet can find the way
Life's trail is rough I know.

When you grow up and realize
What life is all about,
Give me your never-wavering love
Please never leave me out.

William Frank Andrews

TO BECKY AFTER SYMPHONY CONCERT

To Becky A. my little love
My girl who blows the horn.
Remind me of a yesteryear
And some September morn.

September days and lazy dreams
Of summer days gone by.
But wait my love for spring again
And Daddy who is nigh.

Come close to me my little girl
Don't grow so fast away!
I want you ever in my arms
For all of summer's day.

But you say, "Daddy time can't wait.
I'm growing up so fast.
I love you now and always will.
But what is past – is past."

August 14, 1981

From Humble Beginnings

TO BECKY ON YOUR LEAVING FOR COLLEGE (SEPTEMBER 1985)

So you're going off to college;
Little girl we now must part;
And the sadness of this parting
Nearly almost breaks my heart.

Careful now and as you leave us;
Just a token of advice.
Always keep your wits about you
And forever be as nice.

Many times I know you'll stumble –
Find frustration facing you;
Just remember you can reach me.
Come to me – I'll come to you.

Many courses lie before you;
Many roads in life to choose;
Many people; some just like you;
Many though will try to use.

Always keep your goals before you
Remember God is on your side.
Mom and Dad no longer watch you
But we know you'll bring us pride.

William Frank Andrews

Now that Dad is getting older
And I may not be around
I can trust you; this please promise
That you'll never let me down.

Love Daddy

From Humble Beginnings

FOR CHRISTOPHER AND BECKY STEERE (ON THEIR WEDDING DAY JAN. 26, 1991)

I've been thinking 'bout the future
And my mind is hurting so;
As I say goodbye to Becky
Lord I hate to see her go.

But I have great consolation
And my mind was set at ease
When she chose a guy named Christopher
As the man she wants to please.

Now a word or two of wisdom
To my future son-in-law;
Things I've done to keep her happy
From twenty years of being Pa.

Always gracious – always honest;
This my child so many years;
Never brought one day of sadness;
Never caused one day of tears.

Now I see a bright tomorrow;
And the future will be fun
For Christopher and Becky Steere
Will forever be as one!

William Frank Andrews

And when I finally get some grandkids
And they're sitting all around;
I'll be glad Chris took my Becky
'Cause he'll never let 'em down.

Love Daddy

From Humble Beginnings

JESSE'S SHOES

These are the shoes that Jesse wore
White sandals so pretty and neat;
Jesus, please bless these little shoes
And keep our Jesse's feet.

Angels from the throne of God
Surround this child we pray;
And keep her safe from any harm
That ever comes her way.

And little girl with heart so pure
No matter where you roam,
I pray the shoes that you will wear
Will always bring you home.

Poppy, August 9, 1998

William Frank Andrews

JESSE'S MEADOW

Jesse's meadow – cold and snowy
At the breaking of the day;
There is no joy or gladness
Since Jesse went away.

But wait the birds are singing;
They say "This lesson learn –
Spring will come tomorrow
And Jesse will return."

The flowers that are resting
Just beneath the winter drear;
Will be blooming in the springtime
And our Jesse will be here.

And we'll spend some time together
In the meadow sweet and clean;
And our hearts will all be happy –
Jesse's meadow will be green.

Poppy, February 6, 1998

From Humble Beginnings

CHARLES FRANKLIN STEERE

I know a place where I can find
Sweet peace from my travail.
A windswept path that leads through the woods
I call it Charlie's trail.

Charles Franklin Steere a child of my heart;
Your Mom and Dad named you for me.
And sometimes when I walk on your trail
I pretend that you're there with me.

We've walked this path so many times.
We've had good times together.
I want to say I love you Charlie,
Before the stormy weather.

'Cause we all know that storms will come;
But God will see you through.
So don't forget while walking here
To God you must be true.

For I have been weary so deep in my soul
And my heart has been smothered in blue.
Having you Charlie as my loving grandson
Was the light that carried me through.

Old Pops, May 21, 2005

William Frank Andrews

BRENT (FOURTH BIRTHDAY)

A dog named "Snoopy" on a birthday cake –
Today you're four years old.
Lots of friends to share the fun;
A mom and dad to scold.

In spite of all the things boys do
While growing up today,
Your mom and I think you're just great;
We love you anyway.

FOUR years old; so little still –
It seems you ought to be,
Asleep in daddy's room at night,
Tucked in bed with me.

From Humble Beginnings

BRENT (THIRD GRADE)

My little man is eight years old;
And eight is quite enough,
To be the best boy in the school
And all that other stuff.

The third grade takes lots of work
Sometimes they let you play;
The lessons are what it's all about
At ending of the day.

Now girls are cute and lots of fun,
And lots of trouble, too!
They'll get you into trouble
And then they'll laugh at you.

You teacher's smart and very fair;
You'll think she picks on you;
That's not the case for soon you'll see
She wants the best for you.

So get your homework every day
And try to do your best
Then when you bring report cards home
You'll know you passed the test.

William Frank Andrews

TO BRENT AT 15 (ALMOST 15)

Brent you are the last of the line for me;
So son I'm counting on you.
I've tried very hard to leave a good name.
To which you can be true.

Though first you must be true to yourself;
And make your target in life.
Tomorrow will come suddenly –
You'll meet some trouble and strife.

I want you to know I'm very proud
For you to carry my name;
So treat your heritage with respect
And never bring it shame.

For all great men both large and small
Must stand alone someday,
And give account to God above
For talent that came their way.

And you my son will make me glad.
My heart will sing out loud.
I know my name is in good hands,
And you will make me proud.

January 10, 1988

From Humble Beginnings

FOR BRENT AND GINNY

Now my son the time is near us
When you'll marry you a wife,
And the woman that you're choosing
Is the one you'll have for life.

So to you a word of wisdom
From your dad who loves you so.
I can speak these words of wisdom
'Cause I've walked that way you know.

When a man can love a woman
Enough to take her as his wife;
They share the joy of life together
As they walk the road of life.

Sometimes gladness – sometimes sorrow
Maybe fortune – maybe fame;
And sweet Ginny that you're choosing
Will be proud to wear your name.

Always love and make her happy
Sacrifice 'til day is done.
Then these words that I have spoken
You'll be proud to tell your son.

William Frank Andrews

Don't forget that God in Heaven
Made this marriage just for you.
And remember Mom and Daddy
Will be praying for you two.

With love and gladness, June 4, 1994

From Humble Beginnings

PRICE STALLARD

Come sit with me for a spell my son;
Here – scoot up real close by my side.
I'll tell you a story of my oldest grandson,
Who has grown up right under my eyes.

You say you're sixteen – that can hardly be true –
Your childhood is still on my mind;
You've grown up so gentle and handsome to see;
I know you'll make it just fine.

It is easy to see you have set the right course
With your mother and daddy to guide;
So keep walking tall with a confident air,
And you'll always be our pride.

Your future path is all up to you;
You can make it whatever you choose.
So lift up your head and quicken your step
In the end you will win and not lose.

Love Old Pops, April 20, 2005

William Frank Andrews

WELCOME VIOLET

There's a special kind of flower
That is blooming now for me.
God sent Violet in the springtime
So all the world can see.

Violet you are very special;
Number One and Number Eight;
And we'll spoil you like the others.
Nan and Pops can hardly wait!

Little girl I cannot tell you
All the joy or all the pain;
I'll just pray that God goes with you,
Through the sunshine and the rain.

Lord I know I'm growing older;
And I thank you for this child;
And I pray that I can be there;
When daddy walks her down the aisle.

Special love from Old Pops and Nanny

From Humble Beginnings

MY CHILDREN ARE MY GIFT TO GOD

I have known the love of children
Waited by myself alone
When they were out at night together
I've prayed for God to bring them home.

Now I stand at half a century
My children's children now I see
All my years in search of freedom.
Yet no moment comes for me.

Who can say what God has given
Say what miracle is wrought
When we look at life behind us
And we see what love has bought.

To myself I give no credit
God is just and always fair
For the ones that I have given
Unto God for Him to care.

Looking back on life's sweet pleasure
With my wife of thirty years –
What a joy have been our children
Through the trouble and the tears.

For the seed that God has given
Planted, watered sent sunshine
They all wait for God's tomorrow
And I know they'll be just fine.

William Frank Andrews

Victor first son came unto us
In the fall of Sixty-Two.
Today he stands as such a witness
Of just what God can do.

Beth was ours tho' only borrowed;
She came to us in Sixty-Four.
She became our loving daughter
Wish that we could see her more.

Rebecca Ann in Sixty-Seven,
To our house one morning came.
At twenty-one she blesses still
Tho' we'll never be the same.

Brent is ours for this moment;
Sixteen years our baby boy.
These short lines could never tell
All the pleasure and the joy.

So to God I give my future
I accept what be my lot
I have been much blessed by him
And I have not been forgot.

Many times I know I've stumbled
Many times the path was dim
But it looks so very easy
Because I gave it all to Him.

February 7, 1989

From Humble Beginnings

GOING HOME

I want to go back to the hills of my heart;
Back to my Tennessee girl.
Back to the patter of eight little feet –
My wife, my children, my world.

I must go back to *Thornhill* again;
From whence I've wandered away.
Back where the honeysuckle floats in the air;
Out back where the children can play.

There's a lazy old river; a rusty old bridge;
At *Thornhill* that homestead of mine.
And waiting for me my Tennessee girl;
With arms to around me entwine.

William Frank Andrews

THORNHILL (1983)

Thornhill I'm sure missing you –
Your splendid trees and flowers;
I'm coming back to you some day
To while away the hours.

You gave me comfort from the storm
When I was tired and weak.
But now you're gone forevermore
Your comfort I still seek.

You have another master now
But me you'll not forget.
Your trees will live for centuries still
And tell of who they met.

You'll not forget me soon I know;
I gave my best to you.
And every inch of your sweet face
To me has been so true.

From Humble Beginnings

TOMORROW I'll BRING FLOWERS

Somehow I always thought your need
Was spending with me hours;
Now I know it was something else;
Tomorrow I'll bring flowers.

I've always tried to overwhelm
With love and hugs and kisses;
Flowers had no place at all –
They seemed a little sissy.

From this time forward if you can
Please try your best to picture me;
Picking flowers by the way
To fill my lover's plea.

Tho' I still pledge myself to you
I'll sing to you for hours;
I'll love you 'till the grave shall part
But tomorrow I'll bring flowers.

Happy birthday darling

Part 6: War

William Frank Andrews

A CRY FOR PEACE

Now my heart in somber silence cries for sorrow in the
Earth;
All the maimed and dying soldiers ask the question, "Why my
birth?"
Frightened mothers – somber fathers wonder when the word
is said
Will my son come home forever? Will the word come he is
dead?

Leaders falter; offer reasons for the dying and the pain.
Will the peace which seems so fragile ever come to earth
again?
While we bury brave young warriors; innocence still in their
face,
All the world should hide their faces in dishonor and
disgrace.

It seems that war is always with is – every generation knows;
Hurt of death and young men dying; will the tears not cease
to flow?
I will work from this day forward with a dedicated zeal
For a better world to live in and the wounds to help to heal.

From Humble Beginnings

For I have a son so able – and the thought just makes me cry,
If he ever had to leave us; and in some foreign country die.
Madness evermore would haunt me and his mother's mind
would break.
And the world would lose a flower that could never be
replaced.

To you leaders of our nation; to you military men;
Let me calmly give this warning for your thoughtlessness and
sin.
Judgment waits in all its fury if you fail to hear the plea
Of the hundreds and thousands – moms and dads who cry
like me.

*October 27, 1983. Written after the terrible Sunday morning bombing
of the Beirut barracks when those 132 Marines were killed in their beds*

William Frank Andrews

LETTER FROM A SOLDIER

At Franklin, November 30, 1864,
A cry from the midst of the battle;
Mother I'm going to die;
Far from home in a place they call Franklin.
With no one around me to cry.

My comrades around me are falling;
And though I am nearing my death,
Somehow I must write you this letter
Though the battle is taking my breath.

Please say goodbye to my father.
He will miss me most of all.
I am the last of the line for him
But I had to answer the call.

Tell Martha she's now free to marry –
Though it hurts me so bad now to say;
The sons that we wanted so badly –
Another is taking my place.

Away on my right I hear thunder
The guns blasting out in the cold;
But Mother the battle is over
For the weary, the brave and the bold.

From Humble Beginnings

I left you with visions of grandeur –
"We'll settle this thing before long."
But after this battle is over
I won't be around for the song.

Tomorrow they'll bury me at Franklin
With hundreds more by my side.
Forever we'll sleep in the meadow
With only God as our guide.

A new day tomorrow is dawning;
A day with no war and no pain;
And though next week I'd be twenty
The life that I give is not in vain.

Forgive me Mom if my writing
Seems a little restrained.
My hands are cold from the winter
And my sight is dimmed by the pain –

They found him there the next morning.
His letter was there by his gun.
The stretcher-bearer closed out the letter
And signed it "with love from your son."

William Frank Andrews

WELCOME HOME – THE PROUD AND THE BRAVE

Warm winds billow like sunshine
Over the world today.
Crimson clover waves in the wind
And covers the red Georgia clay.

Mockingbirds chirp in the forest
With ecstasy of delight.
Whispering pines tell their happiness
As day fades away into night.

Over the mountain she's waiting,
The candle is burning so bright.
Home from the war is the soldier.
He'll sleep with his lover tonight.

To the one who did not come home:
Deep in the heart of south Georgia
A heart is breaking in fright.
A mother is waiting the return of her son;
His body is coming tonight.

Tomorrow they'll bury with honor
The soldier who did not return.
He gave his life for his country
In a world that never has learned.

From Humble Beginnings

The cadre will honor this hero.
The caisson his body will bear.
America you are so lucky
Because you have soldiers to spare.

But the mother who planted this flower
While he was still in his youth;
Forever will question the reason
Whatever the nation's excuse.

In Athens, Georgia, March 7, 1991

William Frank Andrews

OUR FAMILY (JULY 28, 1996)

If bitter winds should choose to blow
Across our land today;
We'll find a refuge in our God
And choose a better way.

For we are family one and all;
We stand against the tide.
We demonstrate our love tonight;
And in our God we hide.

So mark my words you sons of death
Who choose to wreck and burn,
We curse you for this evil act
And pray that you will learn.

For if you learn that God is peace;
Your torch will turn to love.
Your hate will turn to righteousness
As peaceful as a dove.

Editor's note: "Our Family" was written in reaction to the Khobar Towers (Saudi Arabia) bombing on June 25, 1996. According to Wikipedia (Wikipedia.org), the free online encyclopedia, "This eight story building mostly housed United States Air Force personnel from the 4404th Fighter Wing. In all, 19 U.S. servicemen and one Saudi were killed and 372 wounded."

Part 7: Three Stories

William Frank Andrews

A SHIRT NAMED EUGENE

A few days ago I was looking through my closet for an outfit to wear and became distressed at what I saw. I just could not seem to find anything to wear although I am blessed with an adequate wardrobe. I counted twenty-nine beautifully starched shirts; several jackets; a number of suits and quite a few pairs of mix-and-match pants.

After this quick review of my clothing assets I became thankful and reminisced a bit about my early childhood days when a shirt was a shirt and fit and color match didn't really matter.

I was raised by maternal grandparents who had thirteen children of their own and many times we were the recipients of boxes of used clothing that was sent to us by a Methodist preacher who lived down in Giles County, Tennessee. Brother Moore had a rural congregation that was good about sending clothing to the poor. He also had a son named Eugene Moore who was slightly older and larger than me. At the time I was about eight years old and probably tipped the scales around forty-five pounds. Well, Eugene would wear his clothes until he outgrew them and then stuff them in the poor box to bless some other less-fortunate child.

I remember the day this shirt named Eugene arrived at my house. It came in with a menagerie of other bright-colored but somewhat faded garments. When it came from

153

From Humble Beginnings

the box it was thrust into my hands. Someone said, "Here Frank is a white shirt for you."

It was a little over-sized for me but that didn't matter as I was used to wearing over-sized clothes. What really mattered about this particular shirt was that across the top of the pocket emblazoned in green was the word:

EUGENE

Some mother had lovingly crocheted her son's name in pretty green lettering on my shirt.

I wore this shirt to school and church for a few weeks and the teacher began to call me Eugene. I tried to explain that my name was not Eugene, that was the name of my shirt and I would like it very much if she would stop calling me Eugene. I never did like the name Frank but at least that was what my long-departed mother and daddy had named me. Also, my grandparents continued to call me Frank after I came to live with them when I was about two years old.

I recall the most-sad fate for the shirt named Eugene. It was Sunday morning and the family had made arrangements with one of the older boys to take us to see this preacher in Giles County who had the boy named Eugene who had outgrown the shirt named Eugene. In those mid-forties years a trip to town was an event, but a trip to a faraway place like Pulaski, Tennessee was a lifetime dream. We had planned all week what to wear and the old smoothing irons had been put to work to press all the Sunday clothes that would be needed. Eugene the shirt got special attention for me as it was my only shirt. I was up bright and early with much anticipation and dressed as soon as breakfast was over. I went outside to play until the rest of the family was ready. Well lo and behold what should happen to me and my shirt named Eugene but slip and fall in the slick dew-covered grass? Grass might have

154

William Frank Andrews

been all right except for the fact that the ducks in our yard had nested the night before in this particular spot of grass and these ducks had left their evidence in many places – including the exact spot where Eugene the shirt chose to land.

When I struggled to my feet I knew that my trip was definitely on hold and that Eugene the shirt could be put to permanent rest. However, since there was still a little time left my grandmother quickly washed the shirt and removed all evidence of the ducks and had it dry for me to wear. I remember how sad I felt about wearing the shirt named Eugene to see the boy who had given it to me.

I sure was glad when I outgrew the shirt named Eugene.

April 17, 1989

From Humble Beginnings

SNOWBALL THE ORPHAN LAMB

To those of you who have ever fallen in love with an animal of some kind to have to lose it later and feel the sadness that comes with this loss –

I first found Snowball in a snowy, frozen pasture, although he had no name at the time, in the dead of winter where his mother had deserted him as mother sheep were prone to do on occasion. He was almost dead. At first I thought he was completely frozen to death, but upon picking him up I noticed just a bit of movement. I rushed home with him tucked safely under my thin coat. Upon reaching the warmth of the fire in the living room Snowball began to respond to the heat of my body. I quickly warmed some milk and started dipping my fingers and putting them to the lamb's mouth. His tiny pink tongue responded and within a couple of hours Snowball had gained strength enough to stand on his little wobbly legs.

From this time on Snowball and I were inseparable. On some occasions I even sneaked him to bed with me where we slept cozily together under lots of cover.

As spring came to our farm that year Snowball had to leave the warm confines of the house and go live in the yard. I fed him several times a day with a nipple on a bottle. It was no trouble to find him. All I had to do was walk into the yard

156

William Frank Andrews

and start yelling "lammie, lammie," and he would burst out of hiding with such enthusiasm that at times he would almost knock me off my feet. Snowball grew and grew and began to eat from the green grass that grew profusely in our yard.

To this time no one had ever questioned my ownership of Snowball. After all he was only an orphan that at first would never live so it was just fine if I wanted to waste my time on him – just so long as all my other chores were completed on time. But with Snowball's response to my loving care and affection he now became endangered daily with leaving the farm with the other crop of spring lambs. I tried to tell Snowball to stop getting so fat. All the running and kicking up heels he did would not stop his growth. Soon it became obvious that some plan would have to be devised to hide him from the "bad master" of our farm who would surely see him and suggest a "ride" to the market.

I was successful only for a little while.

One day as Snowball was gleefully playing in the yard the farm master came to see Grandpa on some other business. Upon seeing this robust lamb he asked, "Mr. Sullivan, what is the meaning of this? Have you stolen one of my lambs?"

"No," replied Grandpa. "This little feller was orphaned at birth by his mother and my grandson raised him on a bottle."

"Well," said the farm master, "he should be ready for the market along with the others I came to talk to you about. I'll have a truck here in a few days. What do you say we split the money on this one?"

Grandpa was afraid to say "Well, this lamb would have died without being discovered by my grandson. Why can't we just keep him here as a pet?"

Grandpa tried very hard to tell me in an easy way that Snowball would have to go to market. Nothing he could say would ease the pain of our coming separation. Bitter tears

From Humble Beginnings

could not erase the knowledge that my bouncing inseparable friend would soon be lamb chops on someone's dinner table.

Throughout the next several days I fed and watered Snowball taking great pains to keep him happy. I brushed his wool, polished his small black hooves and loved him daily.

That terrible, fateful day arrived sooner than I thought possible! A large green truck with a great frame bed rolled into the farmyard and at once I knew that Snowball was leaving me. Time will never erase the memory I have of two mournful, brown eyes staring from beneath two slats on that truck and begging, bleatingly for one last bottle of milk from the hand that had once saved him from certain death.

Perhaps death from the cold would have been more merciful.

William Frank Andrews

THE NIGHT THE HOUSE ALMOST BURNED DOWN

Many of my fondest memories of childhood are centered on the years that I lived with my grandparents at the old Walters place on Mallory Road about six miles northeast of downtown Franklin. This old house was a two-story colonial home that was built just prior to the Civil War. It no longer stands to fight the ravages of time as it was totally destroyed a few years ago in order that the rich vein of phosphate that lay underneath it could be mined.

The old house had many good features such as a large banquet-sized dining room where the family gathered for three good meals a day; spacious bedrooms; and tall chimneys on which I used to bounce a rubber ball and pretend that I was the pitcher in the last game of the World Series. The score was usually deadlocked in the bottom of the ninth inning and I was pitching with the bases loaded. Most of the time in my fantasies I managed to retire the other side by striking out the top of the line-up.

In the winter time we heated the house with the wood-burning fireplaces. We never knew what a fire-screen was and many times we had coals of fire pop out and smolder on the poplar floors until someone would snuff it out or kick the ember back into the fireplace. It was surely a miracle that the old house did not burn from those incidents.

From Humble Beginnings

It almost burned one cold winter night but not from the fireplace. I had an older uncle who usually shared the room with me. He came home this particular night a little bit under the influence – a little bit too much to know how unsafe it was to go to bed smoking!

It seems that his carelessness got the mattress ignited and it began to smolder. The more it smoldered the more smoke filled the room. Fortunately for the whole family I was awakened by the smoke.

I immediately rushed to the window and opened it to get a little fresh air into the room. I started to yell at my uncle to get up and help me put the fire out. Well he just could not be aroused! I went flying down the stairs and grabbed a bucket of water and rushed back upstairs and threw it at the source of all the smoke. In the process of putting out the fire I got my uncle soaking wet. Well this got him awake real fast and he jumped out of bed and started to whip up on me!

Looking back on that frightful night I wonder what he would have had me do. Perhaps I should have given him what he really deserved.

April 20, 1989

Part 8: Broke

William Frank Andrews

MY TREASURE SHIP

My treasure ship is out to sea
Seeking balmy skies.
It seems the tempest of the deep
Will give no place to hide.

Somewhere there's a port-of-call
With easy tides and sunny clime.
And when I reach that favored spot
I'll rest a long, long time.

Life is a miracle not a myth.
Waiting is great travail.
And when my ship has found its course
That's how I'll set my sail

Somewhere there are waters still,
Where sandy beaches glow;
There I can rest in peaceful sleep.
And no more troubles know.

I cannot rest until that day;
My soul will have no balm;
Until I reach that distant port
And find the waters calm.

From Humble Beginnings

CHRISTMAS

The shoppers are spending their money
On things for which someone has spoke.
But for me it's just another day
'Cause at Christmas I'm always broke.

I can feel the magic of Easter
With money in my jeans;
Or spend a bunch on Mother's Day
Or maybe Halloween.

But I'm always broke at Christmas.
It's this way every year.
Though somehow Santa does come through,
To bring us Christmas cheer.

Again this year at Christmas
My obligations small
But looking in my wallet
There's no money left at all.

So I'm saying goodbye to Santa
For at least a little while;
And I'll forget it's Christmas,
And pass it with a smile.

William Frank Andrews

For a lot of things I'm thankful
For health and hearth and home.
But Oh, for a little money
So I wouldn't be so alone!

I want to start a fellowship
For Santas far and near;
Who just like me it always seems
Are broke this time of year.

Christmas 1990

From Humble Beginnings

ODE TO A SON OF A B----!

My banker friend the other day
Called me up some things to say.
"Your note is up – the payment's due,
Renew it no! We're calling you."

"Now wait a minute, sir," I said,
"I'm good for it and I'm not dead.
I'll pay you back, I need some time,
To find myself a credit line.

"Sir we've been friends a long long time,
And yes I know I'm out of line –
But things are tough, not going well –
My resources are shot to hell.

"For years I brought my friends to you.
For your good bank I've done my due.
Don't turn your back – my chips are down.
You're not the only bank in town.

"But still you say you've called my note;
You 'hope I strike it rich';
I will some day and you'll still be
The same old SON OF A B----!"

1982

William Frank Andrews

FRANK

I think I like to hear the wind that blows
To me; I'm Frank and me nobody knows –
But I shall be as strong as some oak tree;
Someday someone will shelter under me.

I think that I am one not faint of heart.
Somehow these words to you I must impart.
I'm like a river running quiet and still.
I know I'll find a way to climb this hill.

I'll make my way tho' darkness be my path.
No one can take my breath tho' it's my last.
Although sometimes the darkness covers me;
I shall be strong, so just you wait and see.

Sometimes in vain I try to seek the truth;
And realize that hope is for the youth.
I've come to know this is the life I chose –
But I am Frank and me nobody knows.

From Humble Beginnings

DARK TIDES

I watched the tide as it did break
At rough and ragged shore;
My soul went out to sea today
It shall return no more.

I see so many waves of woe
I cannot find a way.
No matter what my fate may be
My time will come someday.

Cold darkness now surrounds my soul;
The bitter wind is strong.
But I shall pray my anchor holds
Although the night is long.

For up above the darkest cloud
The Son shall reign supreme;
And I who was so near to death
By God can now be seen.

William Frank Andrews

TAKING IT EASY

It's six o'clock in the morning
Outside it's starting to rain.
I'm drinking my first cup of coffee
And it's not helping my pain.

I've raced against time all of my life;
Today I'm taking my ease;
Today I'll worry 'bout nothing,
Today I've got me to please.

I've worked all my life for my fortune;
I've sweated like hell for it all;
I've been friends to the 'big' and the 'little'
And now I'm losing it all.

One thing I hope – a lesson I've learned,
Tho' all of my fortune is lost;
I never will change the way that I am
Whatever the terms or the cost.

I know that someday I'll have money again,
I'll spend it again and not chide;
'Cause nobody yet has worked out a plan
For taking it over the tide.

From Humble Beginnings

BUSTED

I've watched dark clouds on dreary wing
Turn all my skies to gray.
I've hoped against vain hope to sing
The songs I love to say.

All my life has been in vain,
As yet no mark I've made.
I've nothing left except the pain
Of going to my grave.

The winds of hope that once I knew
Now bitter blow my way;
The rest of life for me it's true,
There'll be no better day.

What chance is there at forty-four
To start my life anew –
If only time could change its course,
And make me twenty-two.

Some lessons hard to learn so young,
Make sense when you are old –
There is no friend when you are down
And life has left you cold.

William Frank Andrews

MY PRAYER

Walk with me Lord in these trying hours
Hold me under your wing.
Show me the way from thorns unto flowers
Give me some angels to sing.

I offer to you my heart and my soul;
No one else seems to care.
My burdens are heavy; the path seems so cold
Maybe my heartaches you'll share.

Whenever this shadow has all passed away
The sun will shine once again.
I'll still need you more every day
To still be my kind loving friend.

So walk with me Lord in these trying hours;
Wash my heart with your love.
Give me the strength and give me the power
And give me your grace from above.

Part 9: Writing the Sounds of Night

William Frank Andrews

THE BOTTOM

The bottom is a lonely place.
It has no heart; it has no face.
It has no feeling that is kind,
It has no salve to heal the mind.

So I must strive to reach the top
Until I reach it I shall not stop.
I'll find up there a happy place.
It has a heart; it has a face.

From Humble Beginnings

HELL

Smoldering,

In Earth's rusty crust
Are fires which heat
The very depth of Hell.

Anxiously,

Awaiting strange souls
Whose mortal flesh
Would choose to burn

Eternally.

William Frank Andrews

THOUGHTS FROM A SMALL COUNTRY GRAVEYARD

Today I passed a small graveyard
Near a little country town.
I sat alone in solitude;
The graves were all around.

The whirring sound of a wind-wheel
Designed like Felix the Cat;
No marker for this child-like grave
Except for a small black cat.

Some mother's heart was made to weep;
A father lost a son.
Beneath the clay a small child sleeps
No more on earth to run.

I sometimes wonder as I write
These simple words of verse:
Will someone weep for me someday
As I ride in a hearse?

Or shall I sleep beneath the sod
On silk or satin mat;
In a lonesome country grave
Marked only by a cat.

August 1, 1990

From Humble Beginnings

GENTLE WINDS

Whisper gentle winds of summer;
As you blow across my path.
Lift my sails on moon-lit waters
As the darkness brings its wrath.

Surround my soul ye winds of winter;
With your wintry icy blast.
Though your chill now overwhelms me
The sun will come again at last.

I can see a bright tomorrow
Where no icy winds will blow
Where my soul is safe in harbor
And only gentle winds I'll know.

January 15, 1990

William Frank Andrews

A PATCH OF EARTH

I want a patch of earth to call my own;
Where birds can sing and children can run free;
A spot of ground with trees and sandy loam
A place where Martha can grow old with me.

I want to live what time for me remains
Unfettered by the many chains that bind.
Nor captive to economy's sad strain
I must be free so I can speak my mind.

I've had my fill of chasing earthly dreams;
The will of man with all his evil schemes.
I'll rest a while on earth while here I stay
And trust my God and hope for better days.

November 26, 1984

From Humble Beginnings

I KNOW A PLACE

I know a place where I can write
The lines that I have burning in my brain;
A place where candles flicker soft at night
And on the rusty roof the sound of rain.

The sounds of night I hear outside my door
With pen and paper I can write the sound;
The tapping of the dog's tail on the floor;
Outside the winter night is all around.

The seasoned wood is crackling in the fire
The warmth I need to stir my idle mind;
The ticking of the clock tells me the hour
Is late and I have many thoughts to find.

Someday when all my earthly toil is done
Please take my bones and plant them in the earth;
No matter what acclaim that I have won
I must go back to soil that gave me birth.

November 27, 1984

William Frank Andrews

EIGHTY-SIX CROSSES

I counted eighty-six crosses today
On Highway Sixty-Nine.
Twenty-five miles of death that I saw
Has shocked this heart of mine!

From just shortly west of an historic trace
To Savannah just north of the line;
White crosses mark these scenes of death
Indelibly deep in my mind.

I traveled this highway with fear in my heart;
Each curve brought new sorrow today.
For eighty-six people have died on this road;
No more they'll travel this way.

I cried as I traveled this terrible road;
Tomorrow the governor I'll see.
Maybe somehow some money he'll find
To straighten the curves for me.

Meanwhile this warning my traveling friend;
Please heed each trembling line.
Hold tight to the wheel; keep your eye on the road
If you're traveling on old Sixty-Nine.

From Humble Beginnings

For maybe some crosses I failed to count;
Distracted by curves in the road.
No matter how many; one cross is too much
To stand by the side of the road.

March 20, 1988

William Frank Andrews

MEDITATIONS

Slowly
Tired feet tread
The sands of time.

Only
God knoweth the
Way they go.

Quickly,
Sad eyes scan
The far horizon –

Seeing
There no rest
Except in death.

From Humble Beginnings

DON'T GET HOOKED ON DRUGS

Don't get hooked on drugs my son.
My heart would break for you;
And all your mind would waste away
If this you ever do.

So bright, so fair, your eyes are set
On future plans and dreams;
But watch your step my loving child
'Cause drugs are just a scheme.

I always trust that you will give
Your heart and soul to God;
Then drugs won't seem a better way
As in this life you trod.

So let me spend some time with you
And be your trusting friend;
I'll walk with you and side-by-side
We'll both be better men.

February 26, 1984

William Frank Andrews

THE HUNTER

Very early in the morning
Light has yet to bring the day.
There he is in hushful silence
Stalking yet another prey.

The hunter craves this cold adventure
To outwit the creature fair.
With a cold steel gun of fury
Waiting at the creature's lair.

All the guns in autumn sounding,
Blasting out o'er hill and dale,
For the harvest of the rabbit,
And the deer and duck and quail.

I myself could be no hunter
Though I'm not, I won't condemn.
I could never kill God's creatures –
Not a single one of them.

While I watch in passive silence,
Others kill for sport and fun,
Noble creatures God has given
With a knife and bow and gun.

From Humble Beginnings

THE VOICE OF THE UNBORN

The highway of life was lonesome that night.
She shivered against the wind.
Frail and alone this lovely young girl
Searched in vain for a friend.

I cannot go home – her thoughts turned to death
So easily accomplished today.
Abortion will solve all my problems
And take all my misery away.

The sign on the door said "Open at ten."
The clock in the tower said five.
And deep inside a small voice said "No.
I want to be born and alive."

That tiny small voice must not go unheard,
An advocate is needed today;
To speak for the millions of babies
Who now have nothing to say.

Let's rise up in mass as a nation of love
And close these houses of death;
Or forever the heart of God will be turned
Against a nation of wealth.

William Frank Andrews

A CHOICE OF LIFE

She stood in the valley of the shadow of death;
A young girl afraid and alone.
All of the friends she once counted on
Had vanished; had left her and gone.

So young for this burden; just barely sixteen.
Her parents just could not be told.
They had given the best of their years to her
And now they were helpless and old.

What are my choices? she prayed to God.
Inside her the small baby stirred.
That moment she stepped from the valley of death
And heeded the voice that she heard.

I won't be a part of the slaughter and death.
My conscience would never be sane.
My child must be born whatever the price.
I'll bear it alone without shame.

Now somewhere a child is happy and free –
Because of the choice that she made.
A life – a precious gift of God
Escaped the butcher's blade.

From Humble Beginnings

THE MASTER'S FEET

Sometimes when my soul is dry
And fate deals bitter hands;
My back is pressed against the wall
I pause to take a stand.

I won't be changed by winds that blow
My anchor is well set.
Although the sky is dark today
My God is with me yet.

My strength will come from those I love.
My faith in God is sure.
And though the darkness hovers near
I'll keep my vision pure.

For I alone cannot withstand
This dark and troubled hour.
I'll count on God to see me through
And He will give me power.

So let me lend a word to you
If you are in travail.
Just lay it at the Master's feet
For He will never fail.

October 30, 1989

William Frank Andrews

THE FARMER'S HOME

These are the homes of the farmers,
Where once at the end of the day,
Weary from hours of work in the sun
They rested their troubles away.

Gone are the fires in the chimney;
No more the children will play;
While mothers prepare in the kitchen
The meal at the end of the day.

Work in the morning at daybreak
The farmer and mule would till;
The fertile fields of the valley
For the master's big house on the hill.

Yes, these are the homes of the farmer;
No beauty their mem'ry reveal;
And all of the wounds they have suffered
The pages of time have healed.

Gentle and kind was the farmer,
Their homes my memory knows;
And if there's a heaven for farmers,
I know these farmers will go.

March 23, 1986

From Humble Beginnings

SPECULATIONS

Starlings sprinkle the meadow,
Grass grows green by the brook.
Lovers smile and walk softly
Along the lane just to look.

Brown grows the grass in autumn;
After the first frost of fall,
Shadows are seen in the sunlight.
Turtle doves revel and call.

Cold grows the heart in winter
After the last leaf in fall,
But look to a distant tomorrow
Where turtle doves revel and call.

Life is just one vicious cycle.
The weak are soon sifted out.
I must be strong and not falter
Along life's treacherous route.

Part 10: Reminiscing

William Frank Andrews

REMINISCING

I went back to the country today,
To the place where I was born.
My favorite things had disappeared,
My old house was weathered and worn.

That same little creek I used to know
In which I sailed to sea;
Much smaller it seems; since I've grown up,
But still it beckons me.

Why must I go back again and again
When everything seems so strange?
The world does not stop its turning around;
All things are subject to change.

I beg of you dear Father Time,
Stand still for just a while.
Give me a chance to rest for a spell
As you did when I was a child.

From Humble Beginnings

BAREFOOT BOY

Barefoot boy
With dust and sand
On sun-browned face,

Why think ye
Only of today?

Tomorrow!

With silver hair and
Eyes that sparkle blue
You'll watch gnarled hands

Grow feeble!

Chase the fleeting moments of happiness,
While life is yet young and sweet.
We know with age some things are bitter.

William Frank Andrews

GRANDPA

Grandpa never had a car
Didn't know how to drive;
But he could plow with Kate and Carry,
To make the corn crop thrive.

He bought a tractor just one time
And learned to make it go;
That ended at the gate one day –
Forgot to holler whoa!

Grandpa's nigh to eighty now
He's put the team to rest,
But he is still a hardy soul
For he has stood the test.

Make room our Master for this man,
For he has done his time,
Work was all he ever knew,
He kept the world in line.

When shall I ever see a man
That I can hold so high?
If I can stand as tall as he
I'll need no alibi.

From Humble Beginnings

Grandpa listen when you leave
This Earth of toil and care.
The footsteps that you hear so faint
Are mine – we'll meet up there.

William Frank Andrews

GRANDMOTHER

Grandmother you wiped my tears away
When I was a little child.
When I was frightened late at night
You'd sit with me for a while.

I thank you for the many times
You gave your love to me.
A grandmother's love will never cease
It lasts eternally.

I thank you now for something else –
I wasn't grateful then;
Those switches that you used on me
Were really my best friend.

My heart is saddened now to see
The silver in your hair.
I realize with empty heart
I helped to put it there.

Now I've grown up I realize
What life is all about.
My word you have my grandmother, dear –
I'll never leave you out.

From Humble Beginnings

MOTHER

There ought to be a monument to
The mothers of the world;
For if there were no mothers
There would be no boys and girls.

Without moms there'd be no flowers
In the pretty month of May;
For all the flowers of the world
Are reflections of her face.

I hear the strains of lullabies
From mothers' lips so pure;
The hand that rocks the cradle
Still rules the world for sure.

Your dad may work from dawn to dusk
And then go have some fun,
But mothers never seem to rest,
Their work is never done.

So God when mother's time is up
And she's crossing o'er the tide;
I know she'll find a special place
In Heaven by your side.

May 2, 1990

William Frank Andrews

CHILDHOOD MEMORIES

I was going through some things today;
Some relics from my past.
I came upon a photograph
That makes a memory last.

I wandered back in time again
To when I was a lad.
I thought about my childhood days
The good times and the bad.

This photo that I'm holding now
Is only in my mind;
And tho' someone is missing there
I leave the past behind.

Who is that child that is not there
With smile and golden curl?
A sister that I never knew
Who had a different world.

Tho' sometimes sadness will surround
A boy, a girl, or you –
If you will think on better things
You will not be so blue.

From Humble Beginnings

The sadness comes to make us strong;
Tho' pain may seem severe.
No night is so dark no trial so long
That God above can't hear.

Things could have been different and better
They could have been different and worse
I've given my pain to God above
That's how I'll end this verse.

May 19, 1988

William Frank Andrews

A CHILD FOR A DAY

I want to go back to childhood again
Before I am wasted away.
I must go to sleep in that same little house
And be a small child for a day.

I'll push an old tire down the path to the gate
And over the foot-log again.
Forget all the pressure of living so fast
And be a small child, not a man.

I must go to sleep on a straw bed again;
Or rest in the barn on fresh hay.
I'll tie me a June bug tight to a string
And be a small child for a day.

I'll eat me some peanuts fresh from the pod,
And dig me some worms by-the-way.
I'll cut me a cane pole down in the brake
And be a small child for a day.

Epilogue: Lines from God

If all the goodness of the earth
Was added up to see;
I wonder what my meager worth
To all the world would be.
Oh I've been good a time or two;
Some lines I wrote were fine;
But now the total sum of it
Is maybe worth a dime.
So many times when I was dry
I tried my best to write;
But found the mood was just not there;
I'd waste another night.
And then at times I felt inspired
As words began to flow;
I wondered what the pen would write
As I just let it go.
I hope someday before I leave
This ordinary sod,
I get to write a line or two
That comes direct from God.

December 24, 1990

About the Author

Born in the winter of 1938 to feuding parents who divorced and abandoned him before he was two years old, Frank Andrews lived the hard side of life. The Great Depression of the 1930s had not ended when he came to live with maternal grandparents who were Williamson County, Tennessee sharecroppers.

The shadows of poverty were not great enough to hide the love his new family shared with him. Growing up with a family of fifteen in a sharecropper shack and struggling for a place at the table gave Frank a longing and inner strength to excel. His grandmother had a deep abiding faith in God. She instilled in him this same faith which he has passed on to his children and grandchildren. His grandfather taught him as the last generation of mule farmers to work hard, love your neighbor and to always plow a straight row.

Graduating from Franklin High School in the Class of 1957 Frank continued his education with creative writing studies under Dr. Alfred Leland Crabb. He later attended the University of Colorado while serving in the U.S. Army.

Married in 1959 to Carolyn Smithson, the girl he walked to school in the first grade, Frank came to love her entire family. Her father Walter Lee Smithson was a Pentecostal minister and hard-driving homebuilder who offered good spiritual and financial guidance.

Frank and Carolyn have three children and an adopted niece. Victor is the reliable businessman and president of the family appraisal business. Becky Steere, a multi-talented mother of two, operates The Smocking Loft at The Factory in Franklin.

From Humble Beginnings

Brent, a journalist and published author, is editor of this book. He also works in the family business. Beth Reichstadt lives with her family in another state.

Frank is well-known in local real estate circles. He has served the local association of Realtors as president and the state association as regional vice-president. He currently serves as vice-president of Andrews Appraisal Service, Inc., and is owner of Church Street Realty.

Frank and Carolyn live in historic Franklin in a small English cottage they recently restored. They attend Christ Church in Nashville where Frank is a past board member.

Sponsors

The following sponsors have provided valuable assistance in bringing this book to the public:

Andrews Appraisal Service, Inc.
Franklin, Tennessee
(615) 794-0099

Church Street Realty
Franklin, Tennessee
(615) 790-0806